I have found the A-Z Coaching Handbook a[...] particularly for studying for the ILM Level 5 [...] qualification. The entries are succinct but al[...] can understand in the first sentence what the entry contains. This book is clearly laid out in bullet points that are easy to understand and relate to. There are definitions of topics and an abundance of coaching models, tools and theories within the A-Z, which increases the choice of coaching approaches. I thoroughly recommend this handbook.

Lynn Spurrell, Bath & North East Somerset Council

I'm currently working through my ILM Level 5 Certificate in Coaching and Mentoring, and this book is ****** brilliant! As a rookie coach on a steep learning curve, it is so reassuring to have access to straightforward explanations for the new coaching terms I have come across. If you feel too embarrassed to ask a question about some mysterious coaching terminology you can look it up here first!

Eva Ritchie

Whatever your experience as a coach, this book will pique your curiosity and have you either refreshing your knowledge or introducing you to something new. It provides a foundation in a huge range of concepts and techniques and points you in the direction of anything else you need to take the idea forward. An invaluable source of reference and inspiration which you can access in a trice to get you going.

Caroline Talbott, author of 'Essential Career Transition Coaching Skills'

'What a brilliant idea, all the things that relate to coaching in one easy to find place.'

Kaz White, independent coach.

The A-Z Coaching Handbook

The A-Z Coaching Handbook

First published in the United Kingdom in 2014 by Clare M Smale

ISBN 978-0-9576983-3-8

A catalogue record for this book is available from the British Library.

Cover designed by Angela Jones

Printed and bound by CPI Group (UK) Ltd, Croydon, CR0 4YY

For more details on how Clare and inspired2learn can help you achieve success go to www.inspired2learn.co.uk

Introduction

Welcome to the A-Z Coaching Handbook

This book will explain key terms in coaching

Each entry in this A-Z handbook will give you a clear definition, plus some explanation and cross references where relevant. You will discover a wide range of coaching terms, models, theories and approaches to support and help you. Increase your knowledge and understanding of coaching and take away some ideas to explore further. The beauty of this book is that it gives you quick and easy access to information.

Why should you read the A-Z Coaching Handbook?

- Terms and concepts will be clearly explained
- Become familiar with the language of coaching
- Increase your knowledge
- Develop your breadth of understanding about coaching
- Quickly find out about a tool or technique
- All the entries are suitable for complete beginners
- Dip in and out according to your needs

How to use this book

- This book is divided into alphabetical sections and all entries are arranged in alphabetical order.

- Some entries are brief definitions or descriptions, whilst others explain a tool or theory in a little more detail.

- The A-Z Coaching handbook is designed to give you a starting point for discovering what interests you. It will give you straightforward answers to questions you may have.

- The handbook isn't designed to present theory, tools and techniques in detail or to support these with research findings. There are many books and websites available that already do this brilliantly. Instead, you will be given a unique and wide overview of coaching, with signposts to help you explore further.

- Some of the coaching approaches outlined in this book require certification or specialist training before adopting them with coaching clients.

- Further information about everything listed in this A-Z guide is easily accessible in books, journals or on the web via search engines. You can explore further according to your areas of interest and current levels of knowledge. All entries in this book have been tested to ensure that you can easily find out more information. If a specific reference or source is required in order to find out more, this has been provided for you.

- There are many different schools and approaches to coaching, with much debate about the 'right' way and usefulness of different methodologies and techniques. This book will give you an un-biased overview so that you can investigate your personal areas of interest further. Where advantages and disadvantages have been presented, every effort has been made to give a balanced view.

- This guide is independent and has no specific alliances with training providers, coaching associations, accreditation bodies or different schools of thought. There are no sponsored links, so you can be confident of making your own judgements based on your personal context for coaching.
- Words which appear in *italics* in the main body of text are defined elsewhere.

How to get the most out of this book

1. Skim through for a few minutes, reading a random variety of key words and headings as you go. You might also notice sub-headings, bullet points and diagrams. This will give you a sense of the overall structure and content of the handbook.

2. Dip in and out of this book as much as you like. It is intended as a useful resource that you can return to time and time again.

3. The approaches have been explained simply to make the book easily accessible, irrespective of your prior level of coaching experience. References and signposts for further reading are provided at the end of the book. If you are interested in scientific research and more detail about the approaches and theories covered, you will know where to find out more.

4. Throughout the book you will find reference to the coaching 'client'. This is a general term that is applied to an individual person working with a coach. Some people prefer the term 'coachee', although this word hasn't been used in the handbook for reasons of consistency.

5. Many of the topics, tools and techniques mentioned in this book can be easily applied to working with teams. This handbook isn't specifically designed to support team coaching situations, so just get in touch with inspired2learn if you would like further support with this.

6. You will have ownership over your thinking and learning as you use this book. There are no right or wrong ways to use the handbook - you will discover fresh ideas and possibilities for yourself. Applying your ideas and what you learn is in your hands.

7. Contact us with your suggestions for future A-Z entries and edits. Contact details can be found at the back of this book.

Clare Smale

Aa

Accelerated learning uses strategies to connect right and left brain functions. This includes taking account of a variety of *learning styles*, plus creating a high challenge and low stress learning environment. Georgi Lazanov is commonly attributed with the beginnings of accelerated learning from his psychological research between 1950 and 1980, followed by the books of Howard Gardiner (1983) and Colin Rose (1985).

Accelerated learning principles require the client to take responsibility for creating their learning, absorb many things at once and use all of their senses. The opposite of this (to be avoided) is the client absorbing information, ideas or solutions from the coach. The best style of learning creates new meaning and develops new neural networks so that new electro/chemical interactions take place. At the end of a coaching session, the issue / problem / goal won't be the same as it was at the start, because something will have changed in the thinking about it.

Accountability Coaching should be challenging with measurable results:

- set clear, written, measurable and deadline driven actions at the end of a coaching session
- set clear verbal expectations about change and achievement
- request a verbal progress report at the start of each coaching session - go back to the agreed actions and review progress or

achievement against each step - this relies on clear actions having been set in the previous session

- ask direct and closed questions such as 'did you complete that step? Yes or No?'
- phrase questions in a way that assumes the step has been completed as this avoids confrontation
- accept there might be good reasons why things didn't get done, but don't lower the standard - assume the client is still going to take the step, gain continued commitment and assume future success.

Here are three good questions for creating accountability:

- What are you going to do?
- When will you do it?
- How will you know?

Accreditation Accredited qualifications are reviewed, recognised and monitored by the regulatory bodies in order to make sure that they meet specific criteria and quality standards. Requirements are set out in the Regulatory arrangements for the *Qualifications and Credit Framework*. See also *certification* and *professional bodies*.

Acknowledging is a process that recognises inner attributes which support success, rather than praising a more superficial action which was successful. For example, instead of saying 'your presentation skills were excellent and the feedback has been very positive', the coach would say 'well done for taking a risk and standing up for what you believe in'. Acknowledgement at the level of *values, beliefs, identity* and *purpose* can be very powerful for the client.

ACT coaching model (Guy Reichard)

- Awareness
- Choice
- Trust

ACT coaching model (Stephen Miller)

- Awaken
- Connect
- Thrive

Action plan gives the steps and actions (the 'to do' list) that are needed in order to achieve goals. An action plan gives a structure for tasks and deadlines, monitors progress and makes sure that all eventualities have been covered.

Active listening involves paying full attention to the speaker. It the opposite of half listening or half thinking about something else and it helps to build *trust* and *rapport*. Active listening supports the ability of the coach to understand the coaching system (content and structure of the client's problems and goals) and therefore it improves the quality of questions. (See also *listening*). Here are some practical tips for improving active listening:

- minimise external distractions - put phones or other devices away out of sight and turn them off
- maintain eye contact
- smile to show you are paying attention
- adopt the posture of someone who is listening and also observe the non-verbal communication of the other person

- show encouragement by saying 'yes', 'mmm' or nodding your head
- accept pauses or short periods of silence to allow the other person to think - be comfortable with silence
- *mirror* expressions or words to show empathy or understanding - the more automatic this is the better - deliberate mirroring can communicate inattention, so be careful
- be still – listen with your physiology and avoid fiddling or fidgeting
- say very little out loud, so you avoid distraction from what is being said – be sparing with verbal acknowledgement
- say very little inside your head – let your thoughts come and go and repeatedly re-focus your attention on the speaker
- keep an open mind – wait until the speaker has finished before you decide on your next question or whether you agree or disagree - avoid preparing what you are going to say next
- assume the other person just needs to talk – avoid giving advice or describing similar situations of your own
- ask relevant questions that show you have heard and understood what has just been said
- summarise what you have heard and give the speaker a chance to correct your understanding
- reflect back and paraphrase what the speaker has said to show you understand.
- reflect feelings and the broader message.

Actualisation happens when a person is continually striving to be the best they can be. Actualisation is a bit like the acorn growing into an oak tree or the caterpillar turning into a butterfly. For the client, actualisation is about fulfilling their potential and it is a process that doesn't have an end point. The role of a coach is to create the best coaching environment to nurture potential and enable the client to flourish and this can be done by encouraging clients to:

- develop moments of peak experience, where they are excited about goals or achievements
- explore the meaning of their goals or achievements at a deeper level of harmony
- take risks, be spontaneous and experiment
- appreciate what is currently going well, is abundant in their lives or brings them joy
- laugh at themselves and their faults or failings
- think critically and creatively
- accept that life isn't always fair and that there will be disappointments, uncertainly and frustration
- be independent and resourceful, choosing and pursuing their own direction.

Self-actualisation was first defined by Abraham Maslow in his *Hierarchy of Needs* in 1943 (Figure 1).

Figure 1 – Maslow's Hierarchy of Needs

Affirmations are things that people say to themselves to bring positive thinking into their consciousness. They are positive statements, such as 'I am a success' or 'I am energised'. Affirmations can build confidence, increase self-belief and lower stress. They can also support people by focussing their mind on what they want to achieve. They are widely used in coaching and a good question to ask a client is, 'what is the best thing you could be saying to yourself to achieve what you want?'. The answers can then be developed into one or more affirmations and used to create positive or resourceful mind-sets. Some people write them down or establish a routine of saying them out loud at specific times or situations. Recent research questions the power of affirmations, suggesting that they are too superficial for long term impact because they fail to tackle underlining *limiting beliefs* that might exist (Senay, Albarracín & Noguchi, 2010). A suggested alternative to making positive declarations is asking questions to probe for answers. For example, instead of stating 'I can do this', ask 'can I do this?' or 'what if I do this?' with the intention of creating enquiry, curiosity and creativity.

As a coach you can also affirm the positive behaviours in your clients or their capabilities. Here are some examples:

- thank you for sharing your thoughts with me today
- I know you can do this
- you are clearly very capable when you...

Agenda The needs of the client will inform the coaching agenda and a coach may also need to take into account the needs of the organisation (priorities or strategies) to which they belong. The client brings the agenda and the coach provides the coaching. A formal agenda (or contract) will state the personal, business or organisational objectives that the coaching will address and may also state timings and other factors important to the coaching relationship. Individual coaching sessions should have a clear agenda (written or verbal) and this can either be prepared in advance by the coach and / or the client or agreed at the start of the session.

There is also an informal agenda present in a coaching relationship, as both the coach and client will have their personal set of values, biases and perspectives which influence their motivation, outlook and approach. It isn't possible for a coach to separate or suspend these from their coaching, but instead they can be aware of them and how they might affect their coaching style or judgements. Adopting a recognised code of coaching ethics may support a coach to be *authentic*, coach with integrity and consistency and recognise potential conflict of *values* or unhelpful judgements.

Ah-ha moments occur when new neural pathways are created. When a coaching question stretches the client out of their comfort zone they are more likely to have new insights and moments of clarity (see also *transformative learning*).

Aims can be described as a broad statement of what the client wants and their intentions. Aims paint a brief picture of what the client is seeking to achieve and shouldn't include any reference to the steps or 'how' they are going to achieve it. *Objectives* are the steps the client is going to take and should include a small number of very feasible and clear tasks that the client is committed to in the near future. Objectives will be sensible and precise so that they state exactly what will be done. Aims and objectives are terms that are easily and often confused.

Ambiguity exists where there is no clear meaning. Confusion during coaching can be useful as it promotes learning and new insights. Ambiguity might be a problem if a clear way forward is required or the client is in a stuck state. The coach will decide when to create ambiguity and when to challenge ambiguity, as both of the approaches have their place. Creating ambiguity might mean asking vague questions instead of precise questions. This allows the client to answer without worrying about whether their answer is right or wrong. Ambiguous questions could include words like 'might', 'possibly', 'maybe' or 'perhaps'. This type of question allows for a range of answers and ideas. It can promote creativity and problem solving, without the pressure of presenting the 'right' answer.

To avoid or challenge ambiguity ask 'specifically what?'. This is especially important in setting clear, achievable and measurable actions, for uncovering hidden meaning or identifying clear and precise methods for achieving success.

Not rushing to conclusions can be a good thing in coaching. Ambiguity can be a bit like fog and sometimes finding a quick way to clear the fog and move forward might miss other opportunities hidden within the wider landscape. Delve deeper, ask more questions and be thoughtful.

Amygdala is the area of the *limbic system* of the brain that controls the way we react to events that we perceive as potentially threatening or dangerous. It is the fear centre of the brain, as well as being responsible for other emotional memories.

Analogue communication is delivering a message without words.

Analogue marking Changing your voice or using a non-verbal gesture to mark important elements in a conversation. This can be used with great effect to mark embedded commands or key learning whilst coaching. The technique originates from hypnosis. The conscious mind hears the whole sentence, whilst the powerful unconscious mind hears just the words that are marked out. An example could be *"My friend knows how to worry less about things"* – *'worry less'* can be emphasized by speaking it slightly louder, slower or faster.

Anchor is a learned response to a trigger or stimuli in the environment. Anchors are like the buttons that are pressed within us, creating instant joy, anger, frustration, nervousness and a myriad of other feelings. They happen very naturally in everyday life and can be negative or positive. Here are some examples of different types of anchors (see also *senses*):

- visual – the large golden 'M' of a well know fast food company or the sight of a spider that makes you feel squeamish
- auditory – the jingle of bells invoking a Christmassy feeling or a pop song transporting you back to a particular time and place in your teenage years
- kinesthetic – the Monday morning feeling at the start of the working week or the Friday feeling at the end - wearing different clothes can evoke different states for different occasions
- smell (olfactory) – the scent of freshly cut grass invoking a childhood memory
- taste (gustatory) – the taste of a particular drink or food reminding you of a special holiday.

Applications in coaching:

- uncover anchors that aren't useful and remove, weaken or change them
- set a new anchor to control unhelpful emotions or feelings
- set a new anchor to help create or support resourceful states or emotions, such as being confident, assertive, calm or motivated.

Anchoring as a technique first appeared in the book Frogs into Princes (Grinder and Bandler 1979) and there are now many different approaches and types of anchors.

Andragogy is a set of assumptions (Knowles 1978) about adult learning. These have been adapted as six principles for coaching (Cox et al 2010):

1. Adults need to know what they will be learning as independent learners. Coaching encourages ownership of learning.

2. Adults are self-directed and should be shown respect for what they know and how they prefer to learn. Coaching is free of judgement.

3. Adults have a wealth of prior experience which can be a positive resource or an unhelpful mental model. Unlearning is just as important as learning and one role of the coach is to challenge assumptions.

4. Adults learn when they need to. A coach should understand the client's life situation and adapt their approach and style in order to be most effective.

5. Adults need relevancy and learn best when there is a need to address an issue or a goal. Good coaching will work with short term problems as well as long term development.

6. Adults are internally motivated. Coaching should make a connection between internal needs and values and the results of coaching.

ANLP International CIC is the membership association for NLP Professionals, including coaches. It is a social enterprise, offering a range of membership packages and benefits to help keep skills and knowledge up to date. Membership benefits include networking, publications, marketing support and accreditation.

Association is when a person sees something through their own eyes. This could be a memory brought back to life or a future events that appears as if it was real. The person imagines they are actually in the past or future moment, as if it is going on around them, so that they are fully immersed and are experiencing the sights, sounds and feelings. The opposite of this is *dissociation*. Association is useful in coaching and in particular working with goals, as it helps the client to build positive future experiences. (See also *goals* and *perceptual positions*). Here are some words a coach can use to support a client to associate with their memories or goals:

- As you experience that now….
- As you notice all the benefits that will bring you…
- Step into the future and tell me what you are seeing / hearing / feeling…

Association for Coaching (AC) is an independent non-profit organisation which aims to promote best practice, raise awareness and increase standards across the coaching profession. Members are professional coaches or organisations involved in coaching. The Association is run by a volunteer development team of professional coaches, with membership from 45 countries.

The Association for Professional Executive Coaching and Supervision (APECS) is a British professional body for executive coaches and for the supervision of executive coaches. It offers member benefits such as events and accreditation.

Authenticity means being your own true self. Different definitions mean different things to different people and there may be an element of spirituality for some. The Latin root of the word is 'author', so 'being your own author' is probably the truest definition in the modern sense of the word. Being authentic includes:

- communicating honestly
- being genuine
- you being you
- being real – your true self
- doing the right thing
- being compassionate
- choosing the person you want to be
- having a sense of your values, principles and aspirations.

Authenticity can heavily influence approach, style and confidence as a coach. Supporting others to resolve issues, make decisions and set goals that are authentic for them (and / or their organisation) can be very motivational and inspiring.

Bb

Balance coaching is when the coach helps the client achieve emotional balance, often by shifting a limiting or negative outlook. This is about helping clients understand that they may not have control over all the circumstances in their lives, although they do have the power to choose how to view them. This approach develops a positive mind-set (which in turn can reduce the threat and the stress response) and resourceful steps in the parts of a situation where action is possible.

Barriers to coaching can exist on a personal level or across a wider organisation. Coaching should be introduced gradually in order for it to be truly successful and sustainable. Remove barriers at a rate slow enough to win hearts and minds rather than at a speed which causes fear, is over-evangelical or gives the impression that coaching is a 'here today, gone tomorrow' fad (see also *coaching culture*).

Personal barriers:
- fear of failure
- previous experience
- fear of change
- lack of motivation
- lack of confidence
- not enough time
- lack of trust.

Organisational barriers:

- culture of poor or limited staff development
- coaching not seen as a priority
- low level of coaching skills
- low level of resources and budgets
- lack of time or time pressures
- limited understanding of its value
- resistance from senior management
- transactional rather than *transformational* culture
- lack of integration and a hit and miss approach
- a poor performance focus rather than an excellence focus.

Operational barriers:

- shift patterns
- multiple site working and remote working
- standardisation of models, recording and reporting – not enough or too much.

Basal ganglia are present in their billions and are the habit centre of the brain. They store (and are responsible for) automatic patterns and repetitions. Coaching often seeks to challenge these habitual ways of thinking and behaving in order to form a platform for new habits and patterns. See also *neuroscience*.

Being is the opposite of doing. In a state of being and a quiet mind coaches will be better at avoiding advising, guiding, resolving, leading, suggesting. A good question for a coach to ask themselves is 'what is my 'being' that will enable my use of tools and techniques (the doing) to support the client in the best way possible?'. Being present is often described as the best state for coaching, where the coach is able to focus on the conversation and the client, their mind is clear of distractions and they're not trying to 'do' too much. Being present allows the coach to better engage with listening skills and notice what their client is thinking and feeling, as well as saying.

Beliefs are assumptions that people make about the world. They are generalisations based upon past experiences, both positive and negative. There are beliefs that empower people and those that are limiting. Recognising a client's beliefs during coaching is useful and *limiting beliefs* should be challenged. Here are some examples of empowering and supportive beliefs:

- each day is a new day
- making mistakes helps me to learn
- you've got to be in it to win it
- those who don't ask don't get.

Body language is the observation of physiological signals that people give as a result of their thoughts and emotions. Body language can involve isolated small signals or clusters of signals that are happening together. Body language and its meaning varies from person to person and between cultures, so the value of firm 'rules' is limited. The best starting to point is to spend time noticing the signals and postures for a particular person and then determining patterns for that person and what that appears to mean. This is called calibrating. *Congruence* happens when body language is aligned with the verbal messages that a person gives, for example, they look and sound excited about something, as well as telling you they are excited. Incongruence occurs when the opposite happens, for example a person tells you they are happy and yet other clues in their tone of voice and physiology suggest they are not. Spotting either of these situations is a powerful coaching skill and includes noticing:

- micro-expressions which might pass very quickly
- spatial distances between people
- posture
- rates and depth of breathing
- body movements such as crossing or opening the arms.

British Association for Counselling and Psychotherapy (BACP) is the largest professional body in Europe representing counselling and psychotherapy, with around 40,000 members. BACP seeks to understand, foster and promote coaching as it relates to its core activity of counselling and psychotherapy. Member benefits include publications, networking, professional development and a code of ethics.

British Psychological Society Special Group in Coaching Psychology provides membership benefits which include research, publications, events, code of conduct and ethical principles. Different membership levels are available and include options for those with an interest in coaching psychology as well as those with formal psychology qualifications.

Cc

Calibration is the skill of using verbal and non-verbal communication to be aware of shifts or changes in people. Calibration uses all the *senses* to notices changes in others. It is the same as 'weighing up' or measuring another person's states, preferences and patterns.

Career coaching is useful for anyone looking to change their career, reduce stress at work or shift their work-life balance. Career coaching includes:

- assessment of the professional situation
- evaluation of past, current and future work roles
- increased self-awareness
- use of psychometrics and profiling tools
- skills evaluation
- clarity for future employment goals
- job searching and refining a CV
- managing career risks such as redundancy
- self-marketing.

Cartesian coordinate questions check the *ecology* of a goal and stretch a client's thinking.

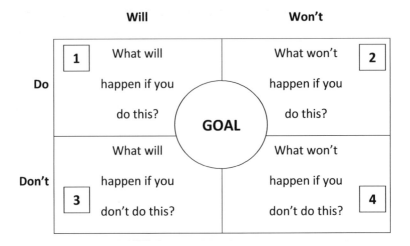

Figure 2 – Cartesian Coordinate Questions

1. Theorem: What will happen if you do achieve your goal? This creates visualisation of the goal.
2. Converse: What won't happen if you do achieve the goal? Allow time for an answer to this question as it helps the client to think about what they might lose (for better or worse) by achieving their goal. Is there anything which will be lost that is important to them?
3. Inverse: What will happen if you don't achieve the goal? This question is likely to bring about some discomfort in considering not achieving what they want and therefore increase the motivation for making it happen.
4. Non Mirror Image Reverse: What won't happen if you don't achieve the goal? This question confuses and can make the client aware of something that was previously hidden. They might gain a fresh perspective.

Certification for coaches is widely available and can be accessed through a huge variety of training providers, professional bodies and universities. The majority of certifications are robust and well regarded, although the coaching industry isn't regulated and some organisations or training providers won't recognise the certifications of others. This has created somewhat of a minefield and it is worth undertaking extensive research before choosing the certification that will suit you best. For example, some training providers' certificates aren't recognised for membership and accreditation of some professional coaching bodies and some professional membership bodies will only recognised their own certification.

In order to have a coaching qualification with transferable credits between learning courses, educational institutions and occupations, the qualification must be accredited through one of qualification awarding bodies in the UK. These are regulated by Ofqual in England, DCELLS in Wales, CCEA in Northern Ireland and SQA (Scottish Qualifications Authority) in Scotland. Many (but not all) coach certifications in the UK are recognised in this way. See also *accreditation* and *Regulatory Qualifications Framework*.

Here are the main routes for achieving QCF accredited coaching certification (ofqual.gov.uk) in the UK:

- Colleges, universities or training providers accredited with City & Guilds
- Universities offering BA, BSc, MA or MSc degrees in coaching
- Colleges, universities or training providers offering Chartered Management Institute (CMI) coaching programmes.

- Colleges, universities or training providers offering Institute of Leadership & Management (ILM) coaching programmes.
- Defence Awarding Organisation (DAO)
- Qulaifi
- CPCAB (Counselling & Psychotherapy Central Awarding Body)
- SFEDI Awards
- Institute of Sales Management (ISMM)
- Mineral Produce Qualifications Council (MPQC)
- Agored Cymru
- Aim Awards

The *Qualifications and Credit Framework (QCF)* is the national system of study units which have credit value. The national credit transfer system consists of eight levels.

QCF Level	School or FE equivalence	University Equivalence	
1	GCSE Grades D to G Level 1 Diploma (Foundation)		
2	GCSE Graded A to C Level 2 Diploma		
3	A Level (AS and A2) Level 3 Diploma / Extended Diploma		
4	HNC	Foundation	University Degree
5	HND	Degree	
6			
7			Master's Degree
8			Doctorate

Figure 3 - The Qualifications and Credit Framework

Championing When the client doubts themselves, the role of the coach is to hold belief in them and help them re-engage with their capabilities. This involves encouraging and supporting the client as well as *acknowledging* their success and achievements. Championing is focused on the past and isn't the same as leading the client by firing them up or energising them towards the future. Championing is about recognising what has already occurred and been accomplished. The most powerful championing does more than point out what has been done and instead praises deeper shifts that have taken place, such as positive changes in self-belief, confidence or resilience (see also *acknowledging*).

Challenge High challenge and low threat help to create an environment which supports coaching and learning. The comfort zone, stretch zone and panic zones of Karl Rohnke's Challenge by Choice model (Rohnke 1989) are often described as three different states that affect learning. In the comfort zone learning may be limited in depth and breadth as the coaching 'plays safe'. Excellent coaching will move a person beyond their comfort zone into the stretch zone for higher order thinking, but without tipping the client into a state of anxiety, stress or fear (panic zone). If there is a perceived threat (this is not the same as being stretched), survival responses in the lower brain (brain stem) will begin to kick in and reduce the effectiveness of the higher cognitive thinking. Making meaning and problem solving will become less effective in the panic zone. The aim of coaching is to stretch the client whilst maintaining their ability to examine patterns, relationships and understanding. High challenge and low stress is sometimes describes as 'relaxed alertness' (see also *parasympathetic nervous arousal*).

Clarifying is when a coach checks their understanding and interpretation, using phrases such as:

- I think that you are feeling…
- so you are saying that…
- I am hearing….

Clarifying is used to check that what the client meant is what the coach understood.

Clean Language was developed in New Zealand in the 1980s and 1990s by psychotherapist David Grove, during his work with trauma patients. It has since been adopted as a coaching methodology and uses a core set of 12 'clean' questions. These are designed to be free of bias, influence or interpretation by the coach in order to explore the metaphors of the client. In clean coaching, the coach will only use the client's exact words and phrases as they ask the questions and the coach will avoid interpreting or reframing anything they hear. Specialist training in this approach is recommended.

CLEAR coaching model was developed by Peter Hawkins in the early 1980s (Hawkins & Smith 2006):

- contract - agree the ground rules and the scope of the discussion
- listen - a reminder to the coach to actively listen
- explore - understand the current situation and open up new possibilities
- action - decide the next step
- review - summarise the ground covered, decisions made and seek feedback.

Clearing is allowing a client to either:

- talk about their frustrations and other negative thoughts and feelings so that coaching can move forward positively
- or celebrate and share successes and achievements ready to move forward.

A client might need to offload something difficult that has happened and vent their anger or frustration and the coach should recognise when this is useful. The coach then provides a structure for it to happen, without hijacking the real purpose of the coaching relationship. The coach holds the safe space (negative or positive) for a limited and agreed period of time (normally 5 to 15 minutes).

The Clearing Process™ is a therapeutic tool created in the USA by Sandy Levey Lunden (certification available) to help a client clear their mind of problems or challenges. It can be used with individuals or groups and requires specialist training. The process involved letting go of the past with forgiveness to make way for a new future.

Closed questions have a YES or No answer. This type of question doesn't develop thinking or exploration. The opposite of this is an *open question*, which allows the client to express themselves in more detail.

Coachee This term is a frequently used alternative to 'client'.

Coaching There are a range of coaching settings. Some coaches specialise in one area whilst others work across a number of areas. Here is the A-Z of the most common coaching genres:

- career coaching – includes choosing work, promotion, retirement planning, coping with job loss and changing careers
- skills and performance coaching - improving the application of skills and knowledge in order to enhance performance or reach specific targets
- developmental coaching – changing behaviour, thoughts, mind-set or outlook
- executive and leadership coaching - a mix of all of the above in order to develop competency as a leader or manager
- life coaching – uses a coaching approach to enhance well being, which may include health, work, home, leisure and social situations
- team coaching – developing team capacity (collective goals and action) through a coaching approach.

Coaching continuum There are a range of coaching styles to suit different circumstances and these are commonly shown on a continuum, with directive coaching at one end and non-directive coaching at the other.

directive ↔ teaching & telling ↔ guidance ↔ questions and reflection ↔ *non directive*

Directive processes might impose the outcome on the client, give advice and offer instruction. The coach does the leading, with this end of the coaching continuum being a common approach in sports coaching. Non-directive coaching (learning to learn) relies on questioning techniques to help the client to develop their own solutions and way forward. In non-directive coaching the assumption is made that the client has the ability to discover their own answers and possibilities and the learner does the leading.

Coaching culture exists when a coaching approach is a key aspect of how everyone in an organisation develops their people and engages their stakeholders. Factors important in achieving a coaching culture include:

- linking coaching to the strategic plan of the organisation
- coaching is led by demand rather than imposed – both for those who train as coaches and those who receive coaching
- creating a pool of well-trained internal coaches and well-respected external coaches
- embedding coaching skills in management development at all levels
- developing internal ambassadors for coaching who will role model effective coaching behaviour
- integrating coaching with HR processes
- encouraging staff who have enthusiasm and talent for coaching as they will help win over those who are more sceptical
- providing continued training opportunities and encourage regular sharing of best practice
- highlighting the positive outcomes, both qualitative and quantitative – part of this involves regular evaluation, collection of case studies and publicising good news stories
- identifying sponsors – staff who have received positive benefits from coaching who will champion the approach at all levels
- coaching upwards, downwards and sideways – anyone within the organisation can act as a coach at any level – cross

traditional hierarchical boundaries and recognise coaching skills independently of other scales or positions

- establishing a common organisational coaching language and internal brand for coaching – a consistency of approach, routines, administration and communication
- supporting individual styles and approaches offered within the pool of internal / external coaches
- encouraging a balance of formal (off line and confidential) and informal (coaching moments or 'water cooler') coaching
- making coaching visible through organisational communication – utilise newsletters, notice boards, displays, intranets or celebration events.

Coaching funnel is a model to show how the coaching conversation narrows as it progresses.

Action

Figure 4 – The Coaching Funnel (source unknown)

Co-active coaching is a coaching model (Whitworth *et al.* 1988) where the client and the coach form an alliance as equals. The coach stays actively engaged with the intention of meeting the client's needs. A significant aspect of Co-active Coaching is to act as a *champion* for the client, *acknowledging* their skills, efforts and achievement.

Cognitive Behavioural Therapy (CBT) and **Cognitive Behavioural Coaching (CBC)** seek to change the way a person thinks and change behaviour by creating a more positive state of mind. Clinical CBT works with thoughts, images, beliefs and attitudes to change negative thought patterns or behaviour. Cognitive Behavioural Coaching adapts this approach for a coaching relationship (non-clinical). CBC addresses issues, problems and blocks to motivation and achieving goals by reducing unhelpful mind-sets, putting in place coping strategies and encouraging the client to take responsibility for themselves. Cognitive behavioural coaches should be trained in this approach, have a background in psychology and receive regular *supervision*.

Cognitive blindness is the unknown unknowns. Another way of looking at it is that we don't know what we don't know. 'Potential' falls into this category (as nobody knows what their true potential looks like until after the event). Coaching works to reduce cognitive blindness, create new thinking and uncover potential. Powerful coaching questions will reveal information, ideas and insights that were previously unknown to the client.

Cognitive effort is the degree to which a coaching client is subjected to deep thinking during a coaching session.

Communication Models Here are three of the best-known communication models (how humans send and receive messages), in chronological order of their development.

The **Linear or Transmitter Communication model** (Shannon & Weaver 1949) has a sender, channel and receiver. The speaker codes the message and speaks, the message is conveyed and the listener listens. The communication has a definite start and finish.

The **Interactive Communication model** (Wilbur Schramm 1954) adds a level of feedback from the listener, so that two (as opposed to one) linear channels are in operation. The speaker speaks to the listener. The communication has an impact (desired or undesired) and then the listener returns the communication. Both communicators share the same message.

The **Transactional Communication model** (Barnlund 2008) states that messages are simultaneously sent and received at the same time and that communication is fluid, simultaneous and involves constant interpretation. Non-verbal feedback is also taking place all the time, so the speaker and listener are both communicating at the same time, although only one of them is talking. This model also introduces the impact on communication of personal interpretation, culture, attitudes and other underlying influences.

Communication can be verbal and *non verbal*. The latter involves the message that pass between people other than spoken words. This type of communication is always present, even if nothing is being said. Verbal communication can be switched off, whilst non-verbal communication is always there, albeit sometimes very subtle. It includes:

- posture
- gestures
- *matching and mirroring*
- facial expressions
- breathing rate and depth
- body postures
- rhythms and fidgets
- orientation in relation to your surroundings.

Various percentage figures have been published from research into the relative importance of verbal and non-verbal clues in communication, with some dispute about the actual statistics. There is widespread agreement on the relatively small impact of words compared to non-verbal messages. Without seeing and hearing non-verbal clues, it is easier to misunderstand the words. When the words create uncertainty, we increase our attention to non-verbal clues. Paying attention to non-verbal communication is very important for:

- setting first impressions
- establishing trust and rapport
- demonstrating enthusiasm and positivity
- detecting congruence (or lack of) in the client
- demonstrating active (or deep) listening.

Compartmentalisation occurs when the client separates different areas of their life and doesn't make links between them. Links could include transferable skills or an appreciation of the way in which something in one area is affecting another area. Sometimes compartmentalisation is helpful, such as when focusing on a work goal

41

and being able to leave personal problems behind. Sometime there are disadvantages, for example failing to recognise that a skill or attribute that is present in a social context might be useful or adaptable to a work context.

Competencies can be defined as a set of defined behaviours or requirements which are important to a particular role or job. Most professional coaching bodies have a set of published competencies and some internal coaching pools within organisations have written or adapted their own. They tend to cover the following broad areas:

- confidentiality and contracting
- ethical and non-judgemental approaches
- collaboration
- facilitating learning and development
- relationships and communication
- professionalism and managing self.

Coaches often use workplace competencies with clients (e.g. role, organisational, management) and this can be useful as a starting point for measuring *return on investment*. Competencies can be used as a scorecard exercise for reflection and development.

Confidentiality It is important to respect a client's confidentiality, as defined by your coaching contract. When coaching within organisations there may be an agreed level of reporting between the coach and the client (and possibly their manager) and this will be stated within the contract. Here are the main reasons for breaking confidentiality:

- risk of physical or mental harm – self and others

- financial or reputational harm to the sponsor of the coaching (the company or organisation)
- issues relating to legal liability or duty of care.

If you believe a disclosure is required, this should be explained to the client. Tell them what you are going to say, when you are going to say it and who you are going to tell. There is a clear risk that trust will be broken and the coaching relationship damaged, although ethically, this is the better option compared to non-disclosure. You may need to seek guidance from a supervisor or professional body.

Conflict coaching occurs where the resolution to a dispute is sought by taking a coaching approach. This can be in a one to one situation or where both conflicting parties are present.

Congruence comes from the Latin verb 'congruere', which means 'to meet together' or 'to agree'. Being congruent is when your values and beliefs, what you *say*, and what you *do* is in harmony. This is the same as physical, mental and spiritual energy being in alignment. Integrity and authenticity are based on the same principle.
A congruent coach is more likely to be trusted and therefore will be able to build rapport quicker. A congruent coach will have their own style, approach and personality which fits with their ethos and values.

As a coach it is useful to notice the clues of incongruence in clients, for example maybe a client's words don't match with their body language. Do they mean what they say? Is there some inner discomfort or anxiety which can be detected? Maybe they were telling you they are committed to making a change and yet subtle clues in their tone of voice or physiology are suggesting otherwise? Spotting incongruence gives the opportunity to ask better questions and delve below the surface of what is being presented verbally.

Lack of congruence within the client may be demonstrated through:

- signs of stress
- inner conflict
- not feeling ready for change
- conflict with others
- spoken words not matching body language.

Conscious gratitude can be described as aliveness, well-being, serenity and joy. What are you grateful for and what is going well, even if you hadn't noticed it at the time? It is the energy of acceptance and harmony. Placing attention on what you want to have happen is the opposite of creating resistance (placing attention on what you don't want). Coaching should support a client to noticing what is going well. It brings into the discussion the skills and attributes that a client could use more of in solving a problem or achieving a goal. Conscious gratitude also creates a more resourceful mind-set of positivity and solutions rather than negativity and problems. Gratitude can help build resilience by learning from mistakes or disappointments. Take forward actions that work, stop doing things that didn't work and put in place new strategies.

Constellations is a specialist facilitated coaching process which creates a physical and spatial map of a relationship or issue. Objects are used to represent the people (or other component parts) of complex issues. The client is asked to position these objects relative to each other and describe the forces at play, the hidden relationships and the paths that exist. New strategies and solutions are then identified. If other people are present in the coaching environment (such as team situations or a training event), they can be used in the place of objects. Constellations is an example of a systemic coaching approach, where the issue might not be clear or relationships are complex.

Contract A coaching contract can be verbal or written. It sets the ground rules and boundaries for the coaching relationship, demonstrates professionalism and ultimately, gives the coach a degree of legal protection should there be a dispute. Written contracts must be fit for purpose and therefore the content and detail can vary between clients. A personal contract might be very different to a corporate contract. Sometimes a contract will need to involve a third party (e.g. a line manager) and be very business-like and at other times something more informal will suffice. Written contracts should include details of

- your fees
- schedule - how often and for how long
- purpose and objectives
- involved parties - coach, client, organisation, HR, manager, coaching agency
- how to handle conflict of interests if relevant
- psychological contract - the unconscious messages and beliefs and the promise to perform and engage
- professional contract – behaviours, competencies, trust, confidentiality

- ending the coaching relationship if required.

Verbal contracts should be established at the start of each coaching session and the value of this is recognised in the first element of the *CLEAR* coaching model. See also *STOKeRS* model.

Convergent thinking seeks to reduce the number of possible answers or solutions. Potentially there is only one correct answer or way forward. This approach includes analytical problem-solving methods which drill down into detail and seek to pin point the best solution (see also *fishbone analysis*). *Divergent thinking* is the opposite to this and assumes there are unlimited possibilities and creative alternatives. Divergent thinking is often used to generate creative ideas and options, followed by convergent thinking to specify precise steps, draw up an *action plan* and communicate a clear way forward. See also *critical and creative thinking*.

Corporate coaching often involves working alongside organisational development (OD) or human resource (HR) colleagues. Common themes for coaching in a corporate environment are change management, team conflict, *aims and objectives*, work-life balance, management and leadership challenges or career development.

Corpus callosum is a thick band of nerve fibres that connects the left and right hemispheres of the brain, transmitting neural messages.

Counselling investigates the causes and roots of problems, whereas coaching mostly focuses on the future and self-development. Counselling is a therapeutic tool to investigate feelings and experiences of the past. The causes and routes of problems can be personal or psychological and sometimes expert *psychotherapy* is required. Counselling assumes that some harm or damage has occurred and a counsellor may also provide information and expertise to support someone to overcome past events and dysfunction that has occurred as a result.

The therapeutic boundaries, training and interpersonal skills of counselling are different to coaching, although both seek to enhance well-being and support clients to make changes in their life. Counselling is likely to utilise a higher degree of empathy than coaching. Both coaching and counselling rely on a non-judgemental relationship of mutual regard and trust for their success.

Counselling and *psychotherapy* are umbrella terms that cover a range of talking therapies. They are delivered by trained practitioners who work with people over a short or long term to help them bring about effective change or enhance their wellbeing. *'Counselling takes place when a counsellor sees a client in a private and confidential setting to explore a difficulty the client is having, distress they may be experiencing or perhaps their dissatisfaction with life, or loss of a sense of direction and purpose'* (The British Association of Counselling and Psychotherapy).

Critical and creative thinking are both helpful for solving problems and for creating new opportunities out of situations that before seemed stuck. Most of us, through conditioning, upbringing and habit, rely on thinking in an analytical or critical way to generate solutions to problems or some new ideas. The characteristics of this type of thinking do not lend themselves to exploring all possible alternatives or looking at options which may appear unconventional or irrational on first appearance. See also *convergent* and *divergent thinking*.

Critical thinking operates in a step by step way. It operates within boundaries. Critical thinking is logical and excludes possibilities through rational argument and therefore results in fewer solutions. It makes assumptions about what is possible. The whole approach is focused towards achieving a result. Once an argument has been reduced to the bare bones, you can go no further with this thinking style. This is a convergent thinking style.

Creative thinking operates randomly and without structure or boundaries. It is designed to generate many alternative solutions. It explores all possibilities, whether conventional or not. Creative thinking does not attempt to limit choices or reduce findings to a single solution. Ideas are explored from many angles and alternatives expand rather than decrease. This is a divergent thinking style.

Cultural differences People will react to coaching differently, depending on what they have been used to. This could be affected by:
- national, religious or racial background
- employment history and the culture of previous or current organisations.

The role of the coach is to recognise where these factors might affect the coaching relationship and to adjust their behaviour accordingly. An open discussion about expectations may be very helpful for both parties in reducing mis-understanding, mis-interpretation or conflict between the coach and client. Geert Hofstede (2004) identified the following 5 cultural dimensions:

- power distance - the degree to which inequality of power is accepted
- individualism - the degree to which personal achievement, rights and success is accepted
- masculinity - in masculine cultures there is more of a marked difference between the distribution of gender roles
- uncertainty avoidance – the degree to which uncertainty creates anxiety and safety is valued
- long-term orientation – the degree to which importance is placed on the future.

In coaching, these dimensions can be used to give a general overview of cultural differences, including what to expect and how to best support or challenge. Recognising culture can help with marketing coaching services to a particular audience or organisation by matching the benefits of coaching to the cultural outlook.

Curiosity can be the biggest pitfall of coaching as well as its biggest strength, depending on the type of question and type of curiosity. People who are new to coaching often seek to uncover a large quantity of information about a client's past or their current context. This is useful for developing understanding, empathy and rapport with the client, although a good coach will quickly move on from this initial stage. A good coach will resist the temptation to be over-curious about the back story and they will seek limited detail about past events. The question 'Why?' keeps the client's focus on the past and within the problem or stuck state.

If curiosity is focussed on the past it can easily become pointless, as the past can't be changed. Here are some examples of how phrasing curiosity about past events in different ways can have a different impact:

- 'Why didn't you complete the project?' This identifies past barriers where it's not possible to go back and make changes. This question creates accusation or blame and will be answered with defensiveness, justification or excuses. It doesn't change anything
- 'How did you manage not to complete the project?' This question uncovers the structure of the problem and shows potential for change or uncovers alternatives.
- 'What is getting in the way of you completing this project?' This identifies future barriers where there is options for action

Gathering learning from past experience is very valuable, so the question 'Why?' has its uses. The skill of coaching is to recognise when it's time to leave the past behind and re-direct a client's focus to future actions and change. Leading questions also stifle curiosity, because they're assuming there is a correct answer and therefore they're not truly curious in their intent. The best type of curiosity will encourage the client to be curious about their future development and ways forward.

Dd

Dancing in the moment Thinking on your feet is a key factor in being a successful coach. Dancing in the moment allows greater flexibility of coaching style and a personalised response to what emerges in a coaching session. A good metaphor for this is freestyle dancing, where the dancer has prior knowledge and experience of steps and moves and so can put these together when the right moment presents itself in the music. Dancing in the moment requires a certain level of confidence, knowing that you can draw upon the right coaching tool, model or approach without having planned it an advance. As with any skill, ease and fluidity develops with practice. The best way to sabotage dancing in the moment is to plan the detail of coaching sessions in advance. Avoid turning up with pre-conceived ideas of how the coaching session should progress. Avoid giving priority to structure and your agenda. Trust and intuition will enable the coach to dance in the moment, with acceptance that until the client starts talking, the coach will have little idea of how the coaching could progress.

Willingness to move is important for both the coach and client. Each moment in coaching can be seen as an opportunity to move – for your client it may be towards new learning, new goals, new solutions, new insights and so on. If the client becomes stuck, the role of the coach is to direct the next step with a question or reflective observation. If the coach, becomes stuck (what to say next), improvise or pause and reflect, in order to allow the next step to come to mind.

Diagnostic tools Identifying the development needs of a client is an extremely useful process and there are many tools for doing this. Once a client has identified and stated their goal clearly, what do they need to learn or develop in order to be at their best? If the goal isn't clear, what are their development needs and how might this help clarify a goal? Sometimes it can be useful to include a feedback process, as a client doesn't always see a development need that others see in them. Diagnostic tools include:

- 180 or 360 *feedback*
- self reflection against *competencies*
- *profiling tools* (psychometrics)
- *wheel of life* (or the wheel of work).

DICE coaching model (Jahnavi Gurjer)
- Discover – listen actively
- Inquire – ask powerful questions
- Challenge – redirect the client towards goals
- Empower – hold the client accountable

Directive and non-directive coaching Directive coaching might include a reduced degree of choice about actions, goals or skills learnt. Directive coaching takes place when team or organisational aims determine direction. Sometimes there might also be limited options of how to achieve what is required. Internal coaching usually has a directive element and the coaching relationship may be linked to line management or project responsibilities. This can affect the power balance of the coaching relationship.

Non directive coaching takes place where the client is in total control of the coaching *agenda*. Personal goals and motivation will be the most important element. External coaches are more likely to be non-directive in their approach as there should be less (or no) conflict of interest. In most non-directive coaching, the coach will be independent and have no power over the client.

DISC personality styles were created by the psychologist William Marston in 1928. He identified four styles:

- dominance
- influence
- steadiness
- compliance.

The psychologist Walter Vernon Clarke (1956 Activity Vector Analysis) and John Greier (DISC personality profile 1958) then created their versions of the DISC psychometric profiling tool which have been adapted by Inscape Publishing (1994 onwards) into the current DISC products . DISC requires a licence and there are slightly different versions on the market.

Disney Strategy (Robert Dilts 1994) is a simple and effective coaching tool with three phases:

1. Dreamer phase - an attitude of anything is possible and nothing is impossible. Modern phrases to describe this are 'blue sky thinking' or 'thinking out of the box'. This phase is about

being fully involved in achieving a goal (first position in the *perceptual positions* model).

2. Realist phase - the plan of action to make a dream come true and the steps the client will take. Step away from personal views and plan the small steps. Act as if the goal is possible and consider different perspectives and reactions (second position).

3. Critic phase - apply logic and analysis. Problems, pitfalls, risks and shortcomings can all be discussed in this stage. Criticise the ideas or the plan, not the people. This is a detached perspective (third position) to remove personal emotions to find alternative solutions to problems.

Dissociation is when a person pays attention to an event, goal or memory from a distance or from the outside. Disassociation is useful in coaching as it can help a client to distance themselves from negative or unpleasant experiences. It helps when seeking different points of view, gaining new perspectives or becoming an effective observer. (See also *association*, *goals* and *perceptual positions*).

Divergent thinking assumes there are unlimited possibilities and creative alternatives. Divergent thinking is often used to generate creative ideas and options, followed by *convergent thinking* to specify precise steps, draw up an *action plan* and communicate a clear way forward. See also *critical and creative thinking*.

Diversity includes gender, ethnicity, socio-economic status, race, age, physical ability, sexual orientation, culture differences and religious or political beliefs. Coaches frequently work with people who are different to themselves, and clients often present issues or problems that are related to working with people who have conflicting values or ways of behaving. Coaching people from a wide range of backgrounds and abilities requires flexibility and a non-judgemental approach and this is recognised within the codes of ethics set by professional coaching bodies.

Coaches can support diversity by working with clients to:
- develop a strategy for the successful management of diversity across an organisation
- develop a shared team identity and behaviour that acknowledges and works with diversity in order to reduce conflict and increase effectiveness
- celebrate uniqueness of ability and personal style
- increase confidence and reduce isolation of individuals and groups who are in a minority.

Drama Triangle (Karpman 1968) is a model that identifies three roles in a conflict situation:
- persecutor
- rescuer
- victim.

Transactional analysis shows how people might switch between these roles.

Ee

Ecology in the coaching context is the study of consequences. What and who else will be affected by actions taken? In science, ecology is the study of the relationship between living organisms and their environmental systems. Human beings are part of human systems. What other people do has an impact on us and our own actions impact upon others. The way we speak, behave and interact with other others has consequences. These consequences might be intended or unintended, positive or negative. Ecology can be explored with clients at any stage of coaching.

EDICT coaching model (source unknown) has been popular for skills development in outdoor sports such as climbing and canoeing since the 1960s. It is an example of directive coaching (see also the *coaching continuum*). A less used version of this model is DEDICT, where an initial demonstration of skills is given before the explanation phase and then followed by a second demonstration:

- explain the skill
- demonstrate the skill
- imitate the coach, instructor or expert
- correct any mistakes
- task - implement the new skill.

Ego states (child, parent, adult) are 'a system of feelings accompanied by related set of behaviour patterns' (Berne 1964). The Ego state functional model explores behaviours and interactions with others:

- Controlling Parent (CP) - rules, should and must.
  Nurturing Parent (NP) – acceptance, nurturing, caring
- Adult –here-and now logic and rationality
- Adapted Child (AC) –complying or rebelling to rules and expectations of parental figures
  Free Child (FC) – spontaneity, creativity and independence from others' expectations

See also *transactional analysis*.

Emotional intelligence is the ability to recognise emotions and manage them effectively. Daniel Goleman (1996) identified the five 'domains' of emotional intelligence as:

1. knowing your emotions
2. managing your own emotions
3. motivating yourself
4. recognising and understanding the emotions of others
5. managing relationships, i.e. managing the emotions of others.

Coaches manage their own emotional intelligence in service of their clients and seek continuous improvement. They are then be able to model the behaviours they are seeking to develop in their clients. Coaching can support clients to explore the impact they have on others at work, home or in another aspect of their life.

Environment The physical coaching environment is largely the responsibility of the coach, although corporate room bookings can sometimes be out of the coach's control. Coaches should be aware of the need for a:

- physical space which is conducive to coaching
- safe space in which to be honest and open
- confidential space
- mind space to reflect and verbalise feelings.

Environment needs will vary depending on whether the coaching is face to face, by telephone or over the internet.

Ethics Coaching relationships are based upon a set of principles and values. The various coaching organisations set out their codes of ethics to guide best and safe practice. Many of these are freely available from their websites. Within organisations, internal coaching pools and programmes normally have their own bespoke codes of conduct and ethics. Codes generally cover behaviour and issues across the following broad areas:

- professional relationships
- contracting, including confidentiality and information management
- conflict of interest and dual / multiple relationships
- safety and well-being
- competence
- self management and continued professional development
- supervision.

European Mentoring & Coaching Council (EMCC) exists to promote good practice and the expectation of good practice in mentoring and coaching across Europe. There are over 5,000 members from 67 countries. They offer membership and coach accreditation with a range of benefits such as networking, professional development and a code of standards and ethics.

Evaluation of coaching tends to be a largely subjective process as the benefits are often behavioural and difficult to quantify in monetary terms. Evaluation provides information on which to base decisions about investment in coaching or for improvement to coaching services. One of the most popular training evaluation models (Kirkpatrick 1976) suggests four different levels, adapted here for coaching:

- reaction - how does the client feel about the coaching? (Surveys, questionnaires, interviews.)
- learning - to what extent has learning taken place and to what extent have attitudes been changed? (Surveys, questionnaires, interviews, skills assessment or tests before and after coaching.)
- behaviour - to what extent has their job behaviour changed as a result of coaching? (360 feedback, psychometrics, behavioural competency assessment before and after coaching)
- results - to what extent have results been achieved? (Goals achieved, profits, morale, grievance rates, return on investment, quantity or quality of output.).

McGurk (2010) suggests the following elements for effective evaluation of coaching:

- develop an integrated approach that utilises both qualitative and quantitative data.
- use reflective notes and scaling data as a raw material for coaching evaluation
- start and end coaching with 360-degree feedback data, psychometrics, learning inventories, team diagnostics, appraisal tools, engagement surveys, HR metrics and key performance indicators (KPIs) - all of these can be used as start and end point measures
- calculate the financial *return on investment* and use it to support other evaluation methods
- collect testimonies of the impact of coaching from clients
- show explicit links between coaching and key business metrics, such as KPIs, organisational targets and service levels
- develop links between ownership and sponsorship, positioning and context, resourcing and procurement, and assessment and evaluation.

Executive coaching specifically supports managers and leaders in organisations. This can be in any role and at any level. This type of coaching frequently focuses on issues involving managing people, but can also include other general leadership behaviours and attributes and visionary goal setting and thinking. The coaching is developmental in that it aims to maximise effectiveness and potential, rather than specifically develop skills and expertise. Executive coaching might include:

- defining vision and goals
- bringing depth and focus to challenges
- gaining clarity and identifying new actions
- a results orientated context
- a thinking partner for support.

Experiential learning is a key part of many learning theories. For example, Bernice McCarthy's *4mat learning* cycle advocates that all learners have the opportunity to put theory into practice and *Kolb's experiential learning cycle* shows learning as a continuous process involving four stages. The role of coaching in experiential learning is to:

- create trust and a space to talk so that the client is actively involved in the experience
- ask questions which will enable to client to reflect on the experience
- encourage and challenge the client to analyse and conceptualise the experience
- develop decision making and problem-solving skills
- commit the client to use the new ideas gained from the experience.

Ff

FACTS coaching model (Blakey & Day 2012) includes five dynamic elements that overlap and interact. It isn't intended to be used as series of sequential steps and was created to support coaches who already have a level of experience:

- *feedback* – give praise and criticism
- *accountability* without blame or shame
- courageous goals - excitement, inspiration and transformation
- tension – the right amount for optimising personal performance
- systems thinking – sustainability, values, ethics and wider change.

Feedback improves self-awareness, gives encouragement or reassurance and provides an opportunity for improving performance. External coaches may not be in a position to give direct feedback, as there may be limited opportunity to observe a person in their day to day working environment. Clients can seek feedback **for evaluation and self-reflection** informally or by using one of the many on line products that are on the market. The results can then be discussed as part of the coaching process. **Effective feedback should:**

- focus on observed behaviour which can be changed
- be objective
- be timely
- be given in private
- be constructive

- create trust and cooperation
- increase skills or improve confidence
- help a person rather than judge them
- offer support.

360 degree feedback tools are widely available. They are designed to collect and report on feedback given by a person's peers, line manager and direct reports. They normally include self-reflection and can also involve clients or other external stakeholders. They provide a useful insight into how others are interpreting an individual's behaviour and for examining the potential gap between how a person perceives themselves compared to how others perceive them. Useful feedback models include:

- AID (actions, impact, desired outcome)
- Feedback Sandwich – good, poor, good
- *Johari Window*
- *Pendleton Model*
- Stop, keep, start
- FEEDBACK (frame the discussion, evidence, evaluation, dig beneath the surface, behaviour, acknowledge positives, identify behaviours/skills to build on, constructive discussion, keep it simple)
- *GROW* (goal, reality, options, ways forward)
- BOOST (balanced, observed, objective, specific timely)
- BROFF (behaviour, reason, outcome, feelings, future actions)
- PEAR (praise, examples, ask, reinforce)
- CEDAR (context, examples, diagnose, ask, review)
- BEEF (behaviour, example, effects, future actions)

- BIFF (behaviour, impact, feelings, future actions)
- STAR (situation, task, action, result).

Receiving feedback as a coach is also of great value, both for continued professional development and also for helping to measure return on investment for the client. Seeking feedback can also help to build trust with a client. Best practice shows that coaches should seek feedback both during and after the coaching relationship. Firstly identify a development goal for the coaching and then ask specific questions (face to face or via a written questionnaire) relating to this. Use a set of professional coaching competencies (provided by various coaching bodies, organisations or internal coaching programmes) against which to assess coaching performance.

Feedback tapering is where the quantity of feedback is reduced as the coaching client moves through the *four steps of learning*.

FERAL coaching model (Glyn Thomas 2007) was created in order to bring *experiential learning* into outdoor education so that less emphasis was placed on instruction (influenced by *Kolb's learning cycle*) and a more non-directive coaching approach could be taken:
- frame the problem
- explore for solutions and experiment
- report back with solutions
- adjust thinking
- learn by applying.

FIRO-B Fundamental Interpersonal Relations Orientation (FIRO) is a theory of interpersonal relations, introduced by **William Schutz** in 1958. This profiling tool is designed to help people to understand their interpersonal needs, working relationships and the way in which they communicate with others. It has six dimensions:

- expressed Inclusion (eI): I initiate interaction with others
- wanted Inclusion (wI): I want to be included
- expressed Control (eC): I try to control others
- wanted Control (wC): I want to be controlled
- expressed Affection (eA): I try to be close and personal
- wanted Affection (wA): I want others to be close and personal with me.

Fishbone analysis is a tool created by Kaoru Ishikawa in 1968 as part of his pioneering work on total quality management in the shipyards of Kawasaki in Japan. It is a *convergent thinking* tool for drilling down to identify root causes of a problem. Very often problems are stated in general terms. By drilling down it can be possible to identify smaller aspects of the problem where it is easier to take action or find solutions. By solving a small part there can be positive knock on effect to other aspects of the problem, therefore reducing the scale of the problem or solving it completely.

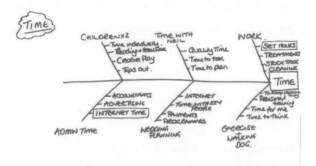

Figure 5 – Example of a Fishbone Analysis

Focus The focus in coaching should always be on client performance, which includes finding solutions, achieving goals and making changes. Coaching supports a client to hold their focus on resourcefulness, opportunities, options and ways forward, which at times of change or feeling stuck, can be challenging. For some clients, shifting from a problem focus to a *solution focus* through self-discovery is the first key step to successful coaching. (See also *accountability*).

Four mat learning was developed by Bernice McCarthy in the late 1970s. She advocates that all learners (irrespective of their learning preferences) are taken through each element in the order shown when teaching new concepts or ideas:

- why - learn by seeking meaning
- what - learn by thinking through ideas
- how - learn by testing theory
- what if - learn by seeking possibility.

Four steps of learning The precise source of this model is unknown, although it is commonly attributed to Noel Burch at Gordon Training International in the 1970s. The four steps are as follows:

- unconscious incompetence – where a person doesn't yet know what they can't do
- conscious incompetence – a person is are aware they're not very good at something – yet! This is the awareness or cognitive stage of learning
- conscious competence – when a person is focused and with practice, they can use the skill / knowledge gained – the associative learning phase
- unconscious competence – the skill / knowledge is being used instinctively and elegantly – the person might not even be aware they are utilising this ability – the acquired or autonomous stage of learning.

FUEL coaching model (Zenger & Stinnett 2010):

- frame the conversation
- understand the current state
- explore the desired state
- lay out a success plan.

Gg

Gestalt coaching developed from Gestalt therapy, which originated in the early twentieth century in Germany and was formalised by Fritz Perls, Laura Perls and Paul Goodman in the 1940s and 50s. An underpinning belief of a Gestalt approach is that a person is acting in the best way possible given their current environment and circumstances and that people adjust in the moment according to their current situation. A Gestalt coach will develop awareness of the current situation so that change follows and most coaching styles adopt this core principle, even without psychological or therapeutic training. In summary, the Gestalt approach covers three broad areas:

- an exploration of what sense the client is making of their world
- raising awareness of how the client is blocking effectiveness
- seeking ways to become more effective.

Goal is a statement of what a person wants, commonly defined as an aim, objective, outcome, output or end point. In Stephen Covey's highly regarded book, 'The 7 Habits of Highly Effective People' (1989), Habit 2 is to 'begin with the end in mind'. Covey suggests the principle that all things are created twice:

- mental creation - the coach asks 'Where you want to be and what you want to create?'
- physical creation and making it happen - a commitment to action and reviewing progress with the client.

There is considerable debate about the value of setting goals. At one end of the scale we are advised that without goals we cannot expect to achieve what we want; that being aimless will lead to drifting through life, achieving less and being unfulfilled. Others question the value we place (at work or in personal development) on goal setting and argue that happiness isn't dependent upon achieving goals, but instead the quality of thoughts 'in the moment'. There is an argument that happiness or contentment shouldn't be evaluated on the basis of what might be achieved in the future (a guess at the best scenario) and that this approach can make unhelpful feelings such as frustration or low self esteem worse.

Goal map is a visual pattern or Mind Map® . It is a divergent thinking (see also *convergent and divergent thinking*) tool that emerged from Tony Buzan's work on psychology and creative thinking. Visual maps are used for generating and recording ideas in a way that mirrors how the brain stores and retrieves information. Each line from the goal in centre of the diagram represents a new idea and extra detail can branch off into sub sections.

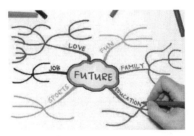

Figure 6 – Goal Map

A goal map can be simple or complex. The visual element is important because the outside world is represented in the mind by mental

70

images rather than words (Pinker 1999). The best maps will include pictures and doodles to illustrate the words and ideas being used. The key words in a goal map are used to trigger images in a person's neurology. The structure of a map shows the associations between words and pictures, mirroring the logic of the brain.

Golden thread is the shared purpose within an organisation. This should be evident not only through an organisation's mission and vision, but also through department, team and individual objectives and these should be incorporated into executive, corporate, leadership or team coaching wherever possible. Coaches will be able to demonstrate clearer *return on investment* if objectives and outcomes can be aligned clearly with the team, department and organisational strategic plans. This includes linking coaching to formal personal development processes or learning programmes (where they exist). The golden thread

- is a shared understanding and 'buy-in' to the vision, goals and values of the organisation
- links to the vision, goals and values within all strategies, plans and policies
- links between vision, systems and people
- is an alignment of thinking, words and actions
- is delivered through individual and team actions.

GROW (Whitmore 2002) is probably the most widely used of all coaching systems. The GROW model was developed in the mid 1980s by Alan Fine, Graham Alexander and Sir John Whitmore. It is based on the principle that peak performance isn't about acquiring additional knowledge, but rather allowing a person to develop and act upon what they already know. Timely, accurate and better decisions produce better results. The GROW model was first written about in Whitmore's book 'Coaching for Performance' and although there are now slight variations being used, the original four steps are as follows:

- goal
- reality
- options
- ways forward.

As with all coaching models, the steps can be used in sequence or with flexibility. An experienced coach will support their client through the model seamlessly, revisiting steps as required. The final step will usually be used to close a coaching session and to create *accountability*, with specific actions and timescales being agreed. The GROW structure is also useful for delivering *feedback*. Here are some adaptations of GROW (added letters shown):

GROW TH – tactics and habits

T GROW - target

F GROW - focus

I GROW - issue

S GROW- strengths

(sources unknown)

Growth mindset is an underlying belief that learning develops talents and abilities (Dweck 2006). The opposite of this is a fixed mindset where intelligence and abilities are viewed as limited. See also *neuron*, and *neuroscience*.

Hh

HARD (Murphy 2010) is model for setting objectives or goals that will stretch a client:

- heartfelt –emotional attachment to the goal

- animated - a vision, picture or movie that can be played in the mind

- required – urgent and necessary

- difficult - out of the comfort zone.

Hay Styles are two profiling tools available from the Hay Group. The Leadership Inventory involves a 180 survey which must be administered by a licensed consultant. The Managerial Styles uses a self-assessed paper-based workbook which can be purchased without a licence. Both of these profiles use the following six styles:

- coercive / directive: gaining immediate compliance from employees
- authoritative / visionary: providing long term vision and leadership
- affiliative: creating trust and harmony
- democratic / participative: reaching group consensus and generating new ideas
- pacesetting: leading by example and accomplishing tasks to high standards
- coaching: focusing on the professional growth of employees.

Herrmann Brain Dominance Instrument is a thinking styles profiling tool invented by William Hermann in the early 1980s. The tool is administered by a licensed practitioner through Hermann International. There are four thinking styles:

- analytical
- sequential
- interpersonal
- imaginative.

Hierarchy of Needs (Abraham Maslow 1943). Needs and motivations constantly shift and change according to circumstances and coaching can help a client to identify their current position in Maslow's hierarchy (see Figure 7). The principle of this bottom to top hierarchy is that the lower level needs to be satisfied before there can be effectiveness at the higher levels. Coaching can support goals and activity to create stability at the appropriate lower level, before the client continues their journey towards higher levels and self-actualisation. Coaching seeks to support and challenge a client at the highest possible level, which is where transformational personal and professional development is most likely to take place.

Some think that Maslow's hierarchy is now outdated because certainty and stability at the lower levels are harder to achieve in the modern world. New thinking suggests that effectiveness from the top down can support constant change and flux in the lower levels. By concentrating on the levels of self-*actualisation*, self-esteem, love and belonging, effectiveness at the lower levels can be achieved in less time. In this instance, the role of the coach is to establish trust and challenge in order to support the client at the higher level. This will enable the client to use their skills and abilities to flourish at the lower levels. (See also Figure 1 and *actualisation*).

Hippocampus is part of the *limbic* system of the brain that helps form and retain short and long-term memories, which is important for learning. It is also associated with focus, sense of direction and motor control. Very specifically, it is responsible for linking memory and smell (see also *anchors, neuroscience* and *senses*).

Holding the environment (also known as holding the space) is a key component of coaching, whether it be a short coaching moment or a full coaching conversation. The 'space' is psychological as well as physical. It means letting go of yourself (e.g. your ego, judgements, solutions or outcomes) so that you are still and 'there for the other person'. A warm, gentle and peaceful approach is a good start in making this happen. By holding the space, the coach gives the best opportunity for the following to flourish:
- curiosity
- flexibility
- playfulness
- reflection
- clarity
- focus
- decision-making
- thoughtfulness
- honesty
- trust.

Holistic coaching is about working with the mind, body and energy system of the client. Tools, techniques and strategies are an important part of coaching and many are described briefly in this book. Holistic coaching is much more than this and takes into account how the coach works differently with each individual client. At the start of the coaching relationship there will be a process of contracting, based on the individual needs of the client. This might take into account past history, future goals, personality type, the agreed focus for the coaching and the type of coaching relationship that both parties wish to establish. Taking a holistic approach will enable the coach to be client centred, plus the flexibility to draw upon tools and techniques that are fit for purpose in each individual coaching relationship. A holistic coach will pay attention to the client's whole experience in life and will be:

- working with the mind
- working with the body – diet, nutrition, exercise, hydration, yoga
- working with energy & the spirit – connection with self, connection with the client and connection with the bigger picture, sometimes described as purpose or spirituality.

Another approach of holistic coaching, is to examine the benefits of coaching not just for the goals achieved, but for the wider benefit of the individual and the systems in which they are a part (such as their family or their organisation).

Ii Jj Kk

Identity is the connection with self and sense of self. The question 'who are you?' elicits answers at the level of identity. Identity can shift during times of change or during lifecycles of an organisation or person. This can create tension, confusion, anxiety and loss of confidence. Re-alignment or identification of identity is often a focus for coaching conversations.

Insights Discovery is a profiling tool for understanding and working with individual and team preferences. The four-colour profile reports on strengths, areas for development, communication style and value to a team. A licence is required in order to administer this psychometric. The four elements will all be present to varying degrees in a person's profile:

- fiery red
- cool blue
- earth green
- sunshine yellow.

International Association of Coaching (IAC) is a global coach certification body with over 13,000 members. The IAC has a set of 'Coaching Masteries' (supported by a code of ethics) which are clear standards and measures for what constitutes the highest level of coaching. These have been designed to be understood in any culture around the world. Coach certification is available, plus networking and learning opportunities.

International Coach Federation (ICF) is a global membership body with over 20,000 members. The basic membership requirement is 60 hours of coach training with strict criteria that must be met. Members are able to use the ICF logo and have access to research, education and networking. ICF provides curriculum standards and accreditation for coach training and different levels of certification for coaches.

Intruding is used when the coach wishes to interrupt a client's thinking or talking. Breaking rapport without being rude is the biggest skill of intruding. A coach would most probably need to do this when a client is spending a lot of time telling their stories or going through endless unnecessary details. Intrusion is especially useful if the client is a serial moaner or blamer (everyone's fault except their own) as the coach might need to cut right across them in full flow, knowing they're not going to pause for breath for quite some time! One way of avoiding intruding, is to specifically frame how much time is available for setting the scene, describing problems or updating progress. This will help the coach to feel less rude when they point out that ten minutes has passed and therefore it's time to stop just there and move on to another phase, such as examining options and ways forward.

The contracting process could include a verbal (or written) discussion about intruding, so that process is depersonalised and the possible reasons for needing to interrupt are explained. Coaching isn't a social chat or an opportunity to offload, although there is a place for this in the coaching relationship (e.g. to build rapport) when managed appropriately. Some clients are brilliant at employing diversion tactics and wriggling out of facing up to things. Being over-polite and over-listening can slow the pace and depth of change. Smile before interrupting and apologise again afterwards, as this will maintain politeness and trust.

Verbal intrusions:

- I am just going to interrupt you here, is that OK?
- Excuse me a second, do you realise that...?
- May I interrupt?
- What does that mean for you?
- What have you learnt from that?
- I don't mean to interrupt, but there's something I'd really like to know...
- Sorry, I've just noticed that the ten minutes we agreed for updates has finished, so shall we move on as we don't want to run out of time for the next part, do we?
- Let me stop you there a moment, I can tell that all is really important you. If you were to focus on moving just one thing forward for the rest of this coaching session, what will make the biggest difference?
- I think I have got side-tracked here, can you explain how this relates back to...
- Yes, and...
- Yes, although...

Non-verbal intrusions:

- raise a hand
- touch the client gently (if appropriate of course)
- break eye contact and look at your watch.

Intuition is sometimes described as a sixth sense. It is a non-analytical response that is sometimes hard to put into words, but is often described as a gut feeling, hunch or a sense that something is right or not right. Intuition is sometimes described as body wisdom, where the coach notices clues and information coming from all areas of physiology, energy and inner self. Intuition comes from different places for different people and it can provide useful insights for the coach or the client. Intuitive coaches ask more questions as they arise in the moment, rather than prepare them in advance. Being open to feeling and being in the moment (see *coaching presence*) will allow better access to intuition. Here are some good questions for working with and developing intuition:

- What are you sensing?
- What are you wondering?
- May I share what my instinct is telling me?
- I am curious to know about...

Johari Window (Luft and Ingham 1955) is a popular technique to help people better understand themselves and their relationships. Self-assessment questionnaires are available and provide a subjective map of personality awareness. The model has wide applications for personal and team coaching.

Figure 8 – Johari Window

- open – the area of honest and open communication - make this area as large as possible for more effective relationships and better team work
- hidden – reduce this area by disclosing information about yourself e.g. small things that show your vulnerability and build trust or things that help others to understand you better
- blind – reduce this area by seeking and receiving feedback
- unknown – what potential do you have? Are you in denial about anything?

Kinesthetic is one of the five representational systems or modalities (visual, auditory, kinesthetic, olfactory and gustatory) and one of three popular learning styles (the other two being visual and auditory). Learning kinesthetically involves movement, touch, discovery, doing and feeling. See also *modality* and *senses*.

Kolb's learning cycle (1984) shows learning as a continuous process involving 4 stages:

- concrete experience (feeling)
- reflective observation (watching)
- forming abstract concepts (thinking)
- testing (experimentation) in new situations (doing).

The Kolb Learning Style inventory is a profiling tool available from the Hay Group

Law of Attraction states that a person's dominant thoughts will bring about results. If thinking is mostly positive then more positivity will appear in life and vice versa. Napoleon Hill and Wallace Wattles were two of the early writers to talk at length about this concept, advocating controlling thoughts and focus in order to achieve success. (The 'Science of Getting Rich' 1910, 'The Law of Success in 16 Lessons' 1928 and 'Think and Grow Rich' 1937.)

Learning There are many different models of learning and a few of the most well known are listed below. See the relevant A-Z listing for more detail.

- *4 Mat learning*
- *andragogy* (Malcolm Knowles 1970s)
- *Kolb's experiential learning* cycle (David Kolb 1984)
- *four steps of learning*
- *multi-stage learning* (Fits and Posner)
- *transformative learning* (Jack Mezirow 1990)

Learning styles There are several different models of learning style. A coach should be aware of their own learning style as this will create biases and will therefore influence how they approach coaching. Their own style may match or mismatch that of the client. Coaching in the style that most closely matches the client will help to support learning, create rapport and build mutual understanding. Although people tend to have a preference, effective learners should have flexibility across all styles and therefore the role of the coach is to support a client to explore and develop in all four aspects. There are many different approaches and opinions on learning styles, with two theories summarised for you here.

Honey & Mumford's learning styles (1992) - Peter Honey and Alan Mumford began their exploration of learning styles in the 1970s, basing their four styles on *Kolb's theory*:

- activist – have an experience
- reflector – review the experience
- theorist – conclude from the experience
- pragmatists – plan next steps

Learning styles profiling tools are available through the purchase of a licence and on a self-assessment basis.

VAK learning styles are based on sensory preferences are derived from *NLP* and *accelerated learning*. Self-assessment questionnaires are widely available. This approach is popular due to its simplicity, with the underlying principle being to present learning opportunities in all three of the VAK modalities in order to develop flexibility and increase sensory awareness:

- visual: responds to visual images and demonstrations
- auditory: responds to sounds and descriptions
- kinesthetic: learns by feeling and doing and experience.

See also *modalities* and *senses*.

Life coach has become a widely used term in personal development to describe coaches who are working with clients outside of workplace issues, although not exclusive of these. The focus for life coaching is supporting clients with personal and professional goals in any area of their life. Common themes include relationships, health, work-life balance, achieving ambitions and being happy and fulfilled. The underpinning mind-sets, skills, knowledge, tools and techniques of the coach are the same as in business or executive coaching, with specialist skills that can be drawn upon to support the areas listed above.

Limbic system is part of the brain that deals with emotions and memories. See also *amygdala*, *hippocampus* and *neuroscience*.

Limiting beliefs are generalisations about a situation that aren't useful, because they hold the client (or the coach) back in some way. They are limiting thoughts that aren't true, but are acted on as if they are true. Sometimes they arise from personal experience (as a child or adult) and sometimes we have them passed on to us (by parents or work colleagues for example). Limiting beliefs can be discouraging and disabling. They often begin with the phrase 'I can't, because...'. Here are some common limiting beliefs:

- I lack motivation
- There isn't enough time
- I'm not strong enough or clever enough
- I'm not good with money
- I shouldn't put my needs before others
- You can't teach an old dog new tricks.

Coaching can help a client to become aware of a limiting belief (pattern of thought) and recognise it as unhelpful. A more useful thought or statement can be chosen in its place and then consciously practiced (or *anchored*) it until it becomes embedded. There are 5 types of limiting beliefs (Arthur 2014) and a key question to ask for each:

Limiting belief	Question to ask
Hopeless	How is it possible?
Helpless	What do you already know about it?
Useless	How is it desirable?
Blameless	How are you responsible?
Worthless	How do you deserve it?

By asking questions, coaching creates uncertainty about old ways or habits of thinking and begins to break them down. As soon as doubt starts to creep into the old limiting belief, there is an opportunity to replace it with something more supportive. (See also *beliefs*). There are many other widely available tools and techniques to help a client overcome or replace limiting beliefs, such as *anchoring, challenging* or *reframing.*

Listening A great coach listens to the spoken word and body language. Listening skills are most frequently described as having different levels:

- Level 1 – listening to the conversation as if fully involved. For example, the client describes a situation at work, the coach remembers as similar situation from their past and starts to experience the memory and have opinions and ideas as a result. The coach has thoughts about the memory and gives less thought to the client's situation as a result. This is also known as first position (see *perceptual positions*).
- Level 2 – the coach is noticing the situation from the client's perspective and is fully associated with the other person (second position).
- Level 3 – the coach is conscious of the client but in a way that is more dissociated and detached. The coach is the observer of the client as well as themselves (third position) and is noticing the dance of the coaching and responding accordingly. The coach is listening to what isn't being said, so will notice the structure of what the client is saying, not just the content. More subtle cues will come to light and coaching questions can be adapted accordingly. The coach can pay attention to their intuition and other reactions.

The **ALIFE ™ model** (Wahl and Stroul) is designed to help the coach to ask better coaching questions depending on what they have heard. When listening to a client, notice aspects of their situation that fall into one of these five areas and then ask questions specific to developing that area:
- authentic – listen for where the client's authenticity has been diminished and they are not staying in touch with the person they wish to be

- leadership – is the client focused on their future, reflective about the past, receptive to feedback and thinking ahead strategically? If not, what questions could be asked to help this way of thinking to develop and be sustained?
- intentionality – focus on the outcome with purpose. If goals are weak and vague, help the client to develop a crystal clear intention
- fear / courage – listen for fear and help the client to become more courageous
- execution – move into action.

Here is another way of distinguishing listening types:
- external listening – listening to the words the client says and how they are said, including VAK
- intuitive listening - what the client isn't saying or the patterns behind what they are saying.

Locus of Control (Rotter 1954) is the way in which people perceive their level of control over events in their life. People with a higher locus of control may believe more in in their ability to change things, influence the world around them and control themselves. Those with lower locus of control may be more passive and accepting (they might believe more in luck and fate, assuming that they can't make a difference). The locus of control continuum is not intended to be interpreted as 'good' or 'bad'.

Both internal and external locus of control have useful and problematic traits. However, a high internal locus of control is thought to bring advantages such as:

- dealing better with stress
- being better able to focus on goals
- increased job satisfaction
- problem solving.

Mm

Mental health can be defined as psychological and emotional wellbeing. Many coaches do not hold a licence or have an advanced education to practice in areas of low mental health, which may create an ethical issue when a client presents with poor mental health. Licenced clinicians who also coach, will be more aware of the issues of abandonment, liability, confidentiality and medication.

The boundary between mental health and mental illness isn't clear, especially for coaches who have no clinical background. In the absence of a diagnosed mental illness, it is important for a coach to have awareness of abnormal or dysfunctional behaviours, low mood, hopelessness, emotional suffering or psychological distress as a starting point. The responsibility of the coach is to ask themselves whether the coaching is within their limitations, monitor the pitfalls and then take ethical action. The coaching relationship must be safe and appropriate.

Buckley (2010) suggests a four-stage process to help guide a coach in making a decision:

1. Recognise that some people may have mental health problems that make coaching inappropriate.
2. Understand the signs and symptoms of mental illness and be able to question the client further when necessary.
3. Understand the ethical, legal, and professional standards and practices.

4. Ask "What next?" Continue coaching, stop coaching or refer for medical help?

Counselling or coaching psychology may be more appropriate for some clients. If the coach has concerns regarding schizophrenia, suicide, harm to others, bipolar disorder or dementia, the client should be formally and promptly referred to a health professional.

Mentoring A mentor is normally a more experienced person who guides or advises someone with less experience. Like a coach, a mentor seeks to bring out the best in that person. Mentoring is a *directive* process, whereby the mentor can impart knowledge, teach skills and share their experiences. They might also actively promote the person they are mentoring (often referred to as the mentee) and introduce them to new networks and opportunities.

Meta view is about standing back and looking at the big picture. By taking a wider perspective, new insights might emerge and wider impacts can be examined. Meta view is useful if the client is stuck in a rut or can't find a way out of something. For example, a coach could ask a client to imagine being in a hot air balloon, floating up above the situation, higher and higher. What do they notice from this new perspective and from examining the whole landscape of the goal or issue? Meta view can also be seen as the general theme of the coaching, such as a time of uncertainty, a time of transition or starting something new (see also *perceptual positions*).

The client or the coach can hold the meta view:

- client – float above the situation and get a wider perspective
- coach – hold awareness of the client's wider life and issues when asking questions.

Metaphor is when something is described as being 'like' something else, either deliberately or as part of the everyday use of language. Metaphor is extremely common and is a constant presence in the language of our thoughts, ideas and experiences. A simple example of a metaphor could be 'I am pruning my expenses', where cutting costs has been likened to cutting back a bush or a tree with loppers or secateurs. Here are a few of the many different ways of working with metaphor in coaching, some of which are simple, whilst others have their roots (excuse the metaphor) in therapy and require specialist training:

- Notice the unique way that each client makes sense of their situation (their *narrative*). For example, in a situation of difficulty, one client might describe the solution as being the light at the end of the tunnel and another will think of it as a new chapter. Adapt the coaching language accordingly to match (rather than mismatch) their metaphor to build rapport.
- Use metaphors that are very different from the client's to develop new perspectives and opportunity.
- Take the above concept a step further and work with the exact metaphor that the client brings by using their exact words and staying in their metaphor. David Grove worked extensively with this concept in the 1980s and subsequently developed *Clean* language. This is now a specialised coaching approach that

supports a client to work with and examine their metaphors (see also *Symbolic Modelling*).

- Tell stories (your own or borrowed) which contain embedded questions, messages or advice to support the client.
- Create new stories which contain key messages or learning for the client.

Mind-body connection The physical body (such as nutrition, exercise and posture) can have a positive or negative impact on mental state. As a coach it is really useful to know this principle and here are some practical applications:

- Encourage the client to act 'as if' they are a particular type of person. For example, if they are lacking confidence, ask them to move, sit or stand as if they are a person who has confidence. By adopting the physiology of a confident person, the mind-body connection principle suggest that the confident thinking and state will follow.
- If an unhelpful emotion begins to emerge from a client, take a short break. When your client gets up from their chair they will change their physiology making it harder to maintain the unwanted emotion. They will take in a deeper breath as they stand up, releasing additional oxygen to the brain. Their eyes will look upwards as they stand, which may help them to move away from emotional reaction and see things more clearly.
- Go for a walk whilst coaching. The forward momentum of walking can support forward thinking and energy feels like it is being more directed into the future. The reduced level of eye contact can make it easier to ask and answer challenging questions. The increased rate of breathing delivers more oxygen

to the brain to promote learning. New environments can release new thoughts and options. The wider field of vision can relax the mind, allow thoughts to pass more freely and create space for new ideas to emerge (see entry for *parasympathetic nervous arousal*).

Mindfulness is awareness of self and the world around us. It is a practical way to notice thoughts, sensations, sounds and other things in the environment. Mindfulness is an ancient Buddhist practice but it is not a spiritual or religious process. Mindfulness is about noticing what we don't normally notice and letting our attention wander in the present moment. Mindfulness when coaching improves listening and increases presence (non-judgement, curiosity and compassion). It can support the client to be more self-aware, reduce stress or anxiety and better manage their responses to life events.

Mindfulness-Based Cognitive Therapy (MBCT) and **Mindfulness-Based Stress Reduction (MBSR)** are two approaches to psychological issues and pain. Both focus on the present instead of the past or the future. Neither are coaching approaches, although coaches may also have specialism in these areas.

Miracle question (De Shazer in 1988) is a *solutions focus* therapeutic technique which is also used in coaching. The miracle question seeks to shift the client into the future so that they think as if their problems have gone:

> 'Imagine you went to bed tonight and when you woke up the problem had somehow magically disappeared and the solution was present…but you didn't know the solution had arrived…

what is the first thing you would notice that would tell you the solution was present?'

The client's answer might tell you more about their problem or what they want. Most importantly, the question helps a client avoid getting stuck in the past causes of the problem. The client is able to focus on what the future will be like and start to think about how they might get there and the first steps.

MiRo is a behavioural profiling tool which provides insights (for self and others) into behaviour, motivations, communication, relationships, making decisions, dealing with change and managing people. Individual and team reports are available. A licence is required to use this psychometric. There are four colour elements, all of which will be present in a person's profile to varying degrees:

- analysing - blue
- driving - red
- energising - yellow
- organising – green.

Mirror neurons help a person to understand the actions, intentions and emotions of others and have been described as 'cells that read minds'. They are found in many different areas of the brain and serve many different functions. Despite recent advanced in neuroscience and MRI imagery, it's still not possible to fully explain how and why this works. They were first discovered by Dr. Rizzolatti at the University of Parma in the 1990s and findings were first published in

1996 (Gallese, Fadiga, Fogassi, & Rizzolatti). Mirror neurons fire when we act or observe the actions of others. They enable us to:

- simulate the actions of others
- recognise the intention of the action of others
- feel what others are feeling, so giving us empathy and shared emotions
- learn by imitation - observing and practising what others do, including mental rehearsal
- connect to other people around us and be synchronised with those people
- develop connections with people by matching thought patterns and movements.

Mirroring can have two meanings in coaching:

- holding up a mirror for the client so that they can become aware of how others might see them or
- subtlety mirroring body language, movements or the spoken words of the client as a way of creating rapport.

Matching and mirroring are supported by the principle that people tend to like people who are like themselves. A sign of natural rapport between people can be when their tone of voice, choice of words, body postures and movements are the same (matched or mirrored). This is supported through relatively new research into *mirror neurons*. In very simple terms, matching is copying the other person in some way (such as both crossing the right leg or breathing in the same rhythm or one person tapping their foot and the other tapping their pen). Mirroring creates a reflection or mirror image of the other person (for example the coach leans on their left elbow and the client leans on their right elbow).

As a coach it is useful to deliberately match or mirror another person into order to generate or deepen rapport. The key is subtlety, as conscious matching and mirroring can be easily noticed and will have the opposite of the desired effect and could break rapport and trust.

Modality is the term often given to the five representational systems (see also *senses*) in which people store and give meaning to our experiences. People have a preference and some people are more flexible in their preferences than others. The modalities (VAKOG) are:

- visual - sight
- auditory - sound
- kinesthetic - feeling
- olfactory - smell
- gustatory - taste.

A sixth modality exists, which is digital. This is where there is no sensory information and a person's experience is expressed in terms of steps, procedures, logic, facts and figures. Most people have a combination of all of the modalities and their preferences may vary in different contexts. The VAKOG words that people use to describe their thoughts are called predicates (see also *senses*) and by paying attention to these words it is possible to pick up clues about preferred representational systems. Here are three very quick examples:

- visual - I have just had a bright idea
- auditory – I have just heard about a new plan

- kinesthetic – I have a solid basis for taking the next step
- olfactory – I can smell a rat in the way this is being set up
- gustatory – I have no appetite for getting involved in the project.

Modelling is the study of how people, groups or organisations achieve excellence. This includes finding out their beliefs, values, skills, patterns, habits, language and strategies for example, in order to create a model and therefore replicate them.

Models are a framework for structuring an effective coaching conversation. They are usually shown as a linear framework. Experienced coaches will start anywhere within a model and navigate in and out of the different steps in the best order for the client. When learning to coach the models are often used much more rigidly. Here is a quick A-Z summary of some of the most common models (each model listed below has its own entry in this book):

ACT - awaken, connect, thrive
ACT - awareness, choice, trust
CLEAR - contracting, listening, exploring, actions, review
DICE - discover, enquire, challenge, empower
FACTS - feedback, *accountability*, courageous goals, tensions, systems thinking
FERAL - frame, explore, report, adjust, learn
FUEL - frame, understand, explore, lay out
GROW - goal, reality, options, way forward
OSKAR - outcome, scaling, know how, action, review

RESOLVE - resourceful state, establish rapport, specify the outcome, open up the client's model of the world, leading, verify the change, ecological exit.

SPECIFY - sensory specific, positive language, ecological, choice, initiated by self, first step, your resources

STRIDE – strengths, target, real situation, ideas, decision, evaluation.

See also *modelling.*

Multi Stage Learning Fits and Posner (1967) identify 3 particular stages of learning. As the learner progresses through these stages they will have gone from unskilled performance with lots of errors to a skilled performance with only very minor errors.

The **Cognitive Stage** is the initial stage of learning. What occurs in this initial stage is cognitive aspects such as understanding the nature and/or goal of the activity or activities. This initial stage requires a high level of concentration and attention. In this initial stage clients may need specific instructions to help them correct errors. The coaching style will be more directive.

The **Associative Stage** is the middle stage of learning where the basis of a skill or behaviour has been established and learned and the client can then start to refine it. This stage requires less concentration than the cognitive stage and errors will gradually decrease.

The **Autonomous Stage** is the final stage of learning where after much practice, the client has mastered the skill or behaviour. In this stage the client can perform with seemingly little effort and few errors. The skill has become almost automatic and requires little concentration and attention. In this stage the coach facilitates the learning situation as the client will have the knowledge to address their own issues and set goal. The coaching style will be non-directive.

Museum of Old Beliefs is a belief-change process created by Robert Dilts (sometimes called the walking belief change pattern). It is a metaphor for storing limiting, unhelpful and outdated beliefs, which the client imagines placing in a safe place in a museum. With the guidance of a coach through the visualisation process, this then leaves freedom for new and more resourceful thought patterns and mind-sets.

Myers-Briggs Type Indicator (MBTI)
measures psychological preferences in how people perceive the world and make decisions. The profiling tool is based on the work of Carl Jung and was developed by Katharine Cook Briggs and her daughter, Isabel Briggs Myers in 1962. There are 16 personality types which are based on the following four dimensions:
1. How you are energised (extrovert or introvert)
2. What you pay attention to (sensing or intuition)
3. How you make decisions (thinking or feeling)
4. How you live and work (judgement or perception).

OPP is the European distributor of the MBTI tool, including the licence to deliver the MBTI instrument and purchase related products.

Nn

Narrative coaching People experience their lives as a series of stories. A coach will have stories in their mind about previous coaching experiences and this will affect how they think and behave in a coaching session (their state or '*being*'). The client will also have stories and a coach can help the client explore these and make meaning of them. The stories of the coach should be irrelevant as they don't belong to the client. Clients are the actor and narrator in their stories and the role of the coach is to be curious about that. Coaching questions explore what the client notices, opens up new perspectives and generates new thinking.

Stories inform thinking, decisions, feelings and actions. Wahl, Scriber and Bloomfield (2008) suggest asking clients these questions:
- What story are you living in?
- How is that story empowering or limiting you?
- What do you need to pay more attention to?
- What are you learning about yourself?

Narrative coaching aims to shift a client's stories about themselves, others and life in general, in order to create new results.

Needs analysis can be used to determine the gap between the existing skills, knowledge, attitudes, behaviours and abilities of the client and those that they want or need in order to function at a certain level. A needs analysis could help by identifying the following:

- skills knowledge or behaviours for development
- expectations and goals
- the need and demand for coaching
- what can realistically be achieved given the available coaching resources
- obstacles or barriers to coaching
- the best fit between the coach and client
- the most appropriate coaching format – frequency, method, duration
- the skill set and knowledge base that is required of the coach
- the required budget and cost-benefit analysis
- the most suitable evaluation approach
- what results can be expected and if/how these can be measured.

Methods of needs analysis include:

- personal development plan (PDP)
- training needs analysis (TNA)
- personal development review (PDR)
- feedback processes
- skills audit / scorecard
- preparation for coaching form
- contracting meetings
- one to one interview.

Neocortex (also called the cerebrum) is the part of the brain responsible for high order functions such as reasoning, conscious thought and language. This area of the brain can generate new neurons (neurogenesis) and as a result the brain has *neuroplasticity*.

Neurological levels (Dilts 1995) is a model which provides a way for people to make distinctions in their experience. The levels provide a framework for understanding an issue or goal and each level uncovers different types of information. The levels can be used to pin point a problem or goal and then specific steps can be put in place, with the result often having a wider positive impact. The levels are most commonly shown as a pyramid hierarchy, although the model is much more flexible than this would suggest and the levels can be approached in any order.

- Environment – where and when
- Behaviour – actions and reactions
- Capability – skills and attributes
- Values and beliefs
- Identity – the sense of self
- Purpose – the bigger picture, mission, vision or spirituality.

Neuron is another term for brain cell. A child is born with billions of these and after birth. Some sources state that no new neurons are created and that the number naturally declines day by day. Modern neuroscience has discovered that neurogenesis takes place from neural stem cells and that these can be optimised by taking on new challenges, learning new things and physical exercise. Neurons connect with each other electrically and chemically and networks are developed. Learning is the creation of new networks. Research on brain plasticity has shown that connectivity between neurons can change with experience and actions taken. With practice, neural networks grow new connections, strengthen existing ones, and build insulation that speeds transmission of impulses.

Neuroplasticity is the brain's ability to change and reorganise over time. Connections can become stronger (through repetition or reinforcement) or weaker (through under use).

Neuroscience is the study of the nervous system and brain structure. Neuroscience has evolved more recently than coaching and is beginning to provide the evidence (through MRI technology) that supports what coaches have instinctively known to be successful. The application of neuroscience research into coaching includes:

- Neuroplasticity – the brain is adaptable and can change with effort and intention. This is commonly referred to as 'rewiring thoughts'.
- New neural pathways can be created with new thinking. The more a pathway is used, the stronger it becomes. Each time an action is repeated, a fatty covering called myelin coats the neural pathway, making connections stronger.
- There are trillions of possible neural connections. Some of them are effective habits and behaviours, whilst others are limiting beliefs and ineffective strategies. Unused connections are a person's potential.
- A person's default setting is to neurological pathways that are already developed, so change requires focus, support, intention and effort. Coaching offers this and can help a client to re-wire their brain for greater effectiveness.

- Research using MRI scans shows enhanced activity in brain areas associated with learning and behavioural change when a coach is open, compassionate, and helps the client focus on a positive future. This activity is not present when the coach focuses on their client's failings, has an answer for them already, and is judgmental (Boyatzis and Jack, 2010).

Neuro Linguistic Programming (NLP) originated in California in the early 1970s and has since become widespread in its applications to coaching. Many coaches have a level of NLP training and many NLP specialists practise as coaches. The four pillars (underlying principles) of NLP are:

- knowing the outcome (the goal)
- sensory acuity - noticing subtle communication cues and messages
- flexibility – working with a variety of tools and approaches to meet a client's needs
- rapport – creating the best coaching relationship and engendering trust.

These four pillars clearly apply to effective coaching practice. NLP offers coaches a huge variety of tools, techniques and processes. Some of these are unique to NLP and others draw upon recognised psychological and cognitive theory.

Non-attachment is the ability of the coach to keep themselves out of the client's way, with a minimal level of influence or interference. Attachment happens when the coach needs their client in some way in order to be fulfilled, for example for friendship or positive feedback.

Non-attachment allows the client to follow their own path and requires the coach to let go.

Non-attachment can also be applied to goals and is similar to a Taoist approach and *mindfulness*, both of which suggest letting go of goals to some extent, so that a desired outcome can evolve more naturally. There is an argument that attachment to goals can cause too much focus and lack of awareness of other opportunities, plus self-imposed stress, pain or dissatisfaction if the path towards a goals doesn't work as planned. Non attachment reduces distraction and creates freedom.

Non-verbal communication includes:
- posture
- gestures
- matching and mirroring
- facial expressions
- breathing rate and depth
- body postures and body language
- rhythms and fidgets
- orientation in relation to the surroundings.

Albert Mehrabian is well known for his work on communication and the commonly quoted statistics from his research in 1967 are:
- 7% of message pertaining to feelings and attitudes is in the words that are spoken
- 38% of message pertaining to feelings and attitudes is paralinguistic (the way that the words are said such as tone of voice)

- 55% of message pertaining to feelings and attitudes is in facial expression.

Mehrabian's findings mean that, as a coach, if you focus heavily on listening to the words you are hearing, there is a good chance that you are missing big non-verbal clues as to how your client is feeling and their attitudes. As a result, your questions may be less insightful and the potential for high impact coaching diminishes. The statistics above are often misquoted as relating to any communication, whereas the research conducted looked specifically at how people communicated when talking about their feelings and attitudes.

Objectives are the steps the client is going to take and should include a small number of very feasible and clear tasks that the client is committed to in the near future. Objectives will be sensible and precise so that they state exactly what will be done. Aims and objectives are terms that are easily and often confused. *Aims* are the broad statements of what the client wants and their intentions. Aims paint a brief picture of what the client is seeking to achieve and shouldn't include any reference to the steps or 'how' they are going to achieve it.

Open questions have no right or wrong answer and require a person to think analytically or creatively in order to create meaning. Here are a few examples:

- What do you think about...?
- Can you explain...?
- What would happen if..?
- When you say that, what do you mean?
- I'd be interest to know...
- What could you do?

Ontology is the study of being, which can be described as the interaction of language, emotions and body. **Ontological coaching** creates a shift in a person's way of being in a way that is consistent with their goals and future desires. This type of coaching has emerged from philosophy rather than psychology and aims to create a change in all three areas of language, body and emotion. Ontological coaching stems from the work of a number of Chileans in the 1980s (Humberto Maturana, Fernando Flores and Rafael Echeverria). Many coaches will be working with all of these three areas (language, emotions and body) already, without even realising that it exists as a distinct and robust approach. Certified ontological coach training is available.

OSKAR coaching model was developed by Mark McKergow and Paul Z Jackson (2006), specifically using the *solutions focus* approach.

- outcome – the difference the client wants to see as a result of the coaching
- scaling – where does the client rate themselves now in relation to the outcome, on a scale of 1 to 10
- know how – what already works or what does the client already know? A solutions focus rather than problem focus.
- affirm and action – the coach affirms the positive qualities of the client and then the client develops their next steps
- review – at the end of the session seek feedback and summarise - in the next session find out (and build on) what's working.

Pp

Paraphrasing is when the coach tells the client what they think they are hearing. When a coach paraphrases, they extract the meaning and reflect it back to the client in their words, not the client's. It's not the same as summarising, which is about repeating the key points or ideas without all the detail that came with them.

Parasympathetic nervous arousal (PNA or PSNA) is a healthy state of comfort and relaxation where the body rests, digests and restores itself. Heart rate, blood pressure and temperature all drop, peripheral vision increases, endorphins are released and processing of thoughts and levels of creativity increase. This is a useful and resourceful state or way of 'being' for both the coach and client. The opposite of this is *sympathetic nervous arousal* (SNA).

Peer coaching is the mutual coaching that can be offered between peers at a similar level in an organisation or situation. It is popular due to its affordability and the mutual understanding of the work (or life) context that is the focus for the coaching relationship.

Pendelton feedback model (Pendleton et al 1984):

- the client identifies his or her own strengths
- the coach reinforces these and adds further strengths
- the client is asked to identify areas for improvement
- the coach reinforces these, adding further areas if necessary, ensuring constructive suggestions are given for improvement.

Perceptual positions is a technique that involves the skill of adopting more points of view than your own:

- first position – the coach or client is fully involved; a position of personal strength - the downside is that you might lack understanding of other person and push to achieve what you want without considering the consequences
- second position - walking, seeing, hearing, feeling and thinking in another person's shoes - aware of the emotions and thinking of others - consider different perspectives and reactions or seek opinion
- third position - an observer of the other two - sometimes this is called the 'friendly visitor from outer space who has just arrived' position or *meta view* - notice more complex patterns and interactions - take a detached perspective and check the wider *ecology* of outcomes, remove personal emotions (client and coach) and find solutions to problems.

This model was developed by John Grinder and Judith de Lozier (1987) who discovered that successful negotiators were able to find a win-win situation through adopting the perspectives of others. The role of the coach is to move the client through these positions, asking questions that develop different perspectives.

Performance coaching places an emphasis on increasing productivity and effectiveness. The focus is on achieving accelerated and measurable results. This approach is common in business and sport, with an emphasis on the psychology of success.

Peripheral vision is the area of vision just outside the line of sight or side vision (Collins Dictionary 2013). Peripheral vision helps to create a state of *parasympathetic nervous arousal* (PNA). The opposite of peripheral vision is foveal vision (having focus). Peripheral vision is helpful in creating relaxation and relaxation is helpful in creating peripheral vision. Both support the coaching process by encouraging clients to open up their view of their world and notice more of what is happening around the edges of a situation. This can in turn provide new insights and ideas and stimulate creativity and divergent thinking.

Permission The client usually gives their permission for a coaching relationship (including format, style, levels of confidentiality) through a verbal and / or written coaching contract. There may also be times during coaching when the client is resistant or defensive in some way. At this point the coach will seek permission to continue, which shows respect and reinforces trust.

Personal coaching places an emphasis on supporting individuals to make changes and achieve goals in any aspect of their life.

Personal development plan is similar to an *action plan* in its structure. A personal development plan will help a client to reflect upon their own performance and then put in place learning opportunities so that they have the best skills and attributes to create and realise what they want. What skills, behaviours and knowledge do they want to develop? What plan can they put in place to ensure this happens?

Physiology is an important aspect of coaching, both for the coach and the client. Experienced coaches will notice *non-verbal* cues (both in themselves and their clients), such as breathing, posture, movements, tone of voice or skin tone. For further information take a look at any of the following entries in this book:

- *mind-body connection*
- *non-verbal communication*
- *matching and mirroring*
- *parasympathetic nervous arousal (PNA or PSNA)*
- *rapport.*

Powerful questions generate creativity, problem solving and new insights. The coach will know when they have asked a powerful question, because there will be silence. The client will go inside to find the answer. (See also *ah-ha moments* and *transformative learning.*) They are often the simplest questions and a few examples are shown below.

- What else?
- What is important to you about that?
- What will make this easy?

Prefrontal cortex is the area of the brain responsible for complex planning, decision-making, behaviours and emotions. It is the last part of the brain to develop and mature. See also *neuroscience*.

Presence is the art of the being in the moment and *mindful* rather than actively 'doing' things or consciously using tools and techniques. Being present requires the coach to trust both the client and the process, knowing that whatever emerges they will be able to respond appropriately and elegantly. This in turn increases the likelihood of transformational and sustainable learning. Presence is a state rather than a skill, although achieving the state can be a skill in itself. Meditation, *mindfulness* and relaxation techniques help, so that stillness of mind and body can be achieved. This requires the coach to trust their professionalism and capability, so that they can react to coaching 'in the moment'. A truly 'present' coach will not be planning ahead whilst coaching, but instead will adjust and respond to what is said and as it happens. Presence deepens trust and intimacy between coach and client.

Present state and desired state Present state is where a goal is stated in terms of what the client wants in the future and there is dissociation from the goal. Desired state is stating the goal as if it has already been achieved and the client is associated with their goal, meaning that they are thinking as if they are in the moment of experiencing it as if it was real. In their mind they have stepped into the future and might be using a visualisation technique to imagine being there. Here is a brief example:

Present State (dissociated) - 'I want to travel to Australia in January next year. I want to see the Great Barrier Reef and live on a sheep station in the outback.'

Desired State (imagined and associated) - 'It is January. I am in Australia. I have just spent a few days at the Great Barrier Reef and I am about to start my journey to a sheep station.'

Problem focus Clients often present a problem as the subject on which they would like to be coached. The problem is then discussed and a goal is set to address the problem. Examples of problem focus questions are:

- For how long has this been a problem for you?
- How do you feel when you think about the problem?
- What impact is this issue having on you?

Problem focused questions generate fewer goal options and steps than solution focused questions (Grant 2012). Many coaches will avoid asking too many problem focused questions on the basis that they reinforce and perpetuate the problem state. The advantages of problem focus questions are that they give the client an opportunity to talk (and for the coach to hear) about their reality of a situation and as a result feel listened to and acknowledged. This is helpful for rapport, relationship building and therefore trust.

Process coaching involves helping a client to be mindful in their experiences, so not only are they aware of their conscious thoughts, but also their emotional and physiological reactions. People take in information through their whole body and therefore, even though it might be difficult to make logical or linguistic understanding, a person's body will be communicating useful information back. This is a bit like having a nagging feeling and not really knowing why, or that something just feels right. *Neuroscience* suggests that the communication received through physiology is processed by the right hemisphere of the brain, which is why rational, logical and linguistic interpretation of that evidence is difficult.

Professional bodies Coaching bodies provides a range of member benefits, including codes of ethics, professional development events, publications, competencies, different membership levels and accreditation options.

- *Association for Coaching* (AC)
- *Association for NLP* (ANLP)
- *Association for Professional Executive Coaching & Supervision* (APECS)
- *British Association for Counselling and Psychotherapy Coaching (BACPC)*
- *British Psychological Society Special Group in Coaching Psychology* (BPS SGCP)
- *European Mentoring & Coaching Council* (EMCC)
- *International Association of Coaches* (IAC)
- *International Coach Federation* (ICF)

Profiling tools (also known as psychometrics) have been developed to measure and label learning styles, aptitude, ability, behaviour and personality. Some of these are designed for individuals, some for teams and a few can be used with both very effectively. Below is an A-Z list of some of the assessment tools most widely used by coaches:

- *DISC*
- Emotional Quotient Inventory
- *FIRO-B*
- *Hay Leadership Styles*
- *Herrmann Brain Dominance Instrument*
- *Insights Discovery*
- *Kolb's learning styles*
- *MiRo behavioural modes*
- *Myers Briggs Type Indicator (MBTI)*
- *Saville Wave*
- *Sixteen Personality Factors (16PF)*
- *Strengths Deployment Inventory (SDI)*
- *TetraMap*

Results are reported to clients numerically, graphically, by colour or through pictures, and in varying degrees of written analytical detail. The cost also varies, with shortened or trial versions being available free on line for a few, whilst most require the coach to be licensed to run the profiling tool and give feedback. All are very useful in opening up a conversation about the client's current behaviours and attitudes (individual or team) and how effective these are in supporting the goal or changes that the client wants.

Provocative Coaching is a methodology created by Frank Farrelly in the early 1970s. A provocative coach uses humour to challenge the client. This can include:

- playing devil's advocate and agreeing with the client's negative comments and feelings
- exaggerating the client's problems and issues

- belittling the client's problems or issues
- pretending not to understand the client
- being direct and to the point
- tempting the client to continue with their negative behaviours
- challenging the client to assert themselves.

The humour and challenge is delivered with a caring and supportive approach (often described by provocative coaches as 'a twinkle in the eye') and mustn't be aggressive, sarcastic or comedic. The provocative approach is designed to elicit new insights for the client by evoking an emotional reaction, such as laughter, anger, irritation or defensiveness. Specialist training in this approach is recommended.

Psychometrics See *profiling tools*.

Psychotherapy Some coaches have a specialist psychotherapy background and qualifications, which equips them to treat the psychological issues that require support from a qualified mental health professional. Psychotherapy is a term which embraces many different areas of psychological intervention. It includes some types of counselling, hypnotherapy, musical therapy and art therapy, plus clinical psychiatry. Coaching codes of ethics state the need for coaches to recognise their limits of competence when contracting with clients and to be clear on the type of coaching with which they are engaging and the boundaries of the coaching conversation in that context.

PURE is a goal setting acronym (Whitmore 2002). Use the PURE model to check that a goal is:

- positively stated and with positive intent
- under the client's control
- realistic and the right size for them to make happen
- ecological and ethical.

Purpose Acknowledging and understanding purpose can be very motivational for coaching clients. Purpose is the reason why a person does what they do and where they place themselves in the society and beyond. It's the force which provides motivation and determination at a level which can be hard to articulate. For some people there is a spiritual or religious element, whilst others describe it as the overall impact they want to have or their intention for how they go about life. (See also *neurological levels*). Ask questions like these to uncover a person's purpose:

- What would you like your epitaph to be?
- Why are you here on this earth?
- What talents and gifts do you have that you can give to others?

Qualifications and Credit Framework (QCF) is the credit transfer system which recognises qualifications and units of learning by awarding credits. Each unit of study has a credit value and the credits can be transferred, giving learners the ability to get qualifications at their own pace. The QCF is jointly regulated by the England's regulator Ofqual, Wales' DCELLS and Northern Ireland's CCEA. (See also *certification, accreditation* and *Regulated Qualifications Framework*.)

Questions In coaching there is a strong underlying presupposition that the client has all the answers within and is the 'expert' about themselves. The role of the coach is therefore to ask questions to help the client to think through options or solutions, make their own decisions and choose their way forward. The job of the coach is to ask questions that help the client to focus on their goals or issues with a different perspective. The best coaching questions help a client to think, feel or react differently, whilst less powerful questions will simply elicit information within the current way of thinking (frame of reference).

A-Z of questions:

- Closed - have a yes or no answer or present a choice between options.
- Commitment - How might you solve this right now? When will you do that?

- Distal - create thoughts for the future, between coaching sessions, a bit like homework.
- Dumb (Whitworth 1988) - too obvious to ask, or are they? What do you want? What is next?
- Future pacing - imagine the goal has been achieved. What is it like to be the person who already does this?
- Incisive - take away a limiting belief temporarily. What if you could not fail? What if time wasn't a problem?
- Leading - these prompt the client to reply in a particular way. For example 'What problems do you have with your colleague?' assumes there are problems and leads the client in that direction. A non-leading question would be 'how is your relationship with your colleague?'.
- Negative interrogation - keeps the focus on the problem and should be used sparingly. Why don't you…? What stops you from…?
- Open - create potential. What are your options? What is your next step?
- Permission - check that it's OK to explore something difficult. How would you feel about exploring this now?
- Precision - directly challenge the client. Exactly what will you do next?
- Proximal - questions about the here and now.
- Truth - gain a deeper understanding. What is the truth here? What is really stopping you?
- Reframing - take a negative outlook and focus on something positive. What is your best attribute that can help you solve this?
- *Socratic* questions look for contradiction or inconsistency

- Why - asking this question requires the client to stay in their old patterns of thinking, which is in conflict to the purpose of coaching. This question is commonly and effectively used in therapy rather than coaching. In a coaching context it can cause the client to be defensive or get stuck in negative thinking patterns. It is a useful question when used sparingly, rather than a powerful question.

Rapport The word rapport is derived from French and means harmony or affinity with another person. Much research has now been carried out into the function of *mirror neurons,* with the discovery that they unconsciously enable people to match and mirror what they observe in others; with our body language and rhythms (physiology) and also spoken language. In simple terms, this means that it is possible to gain artificial but meaningful rapport with another person by deliberately matching and mirroring them, leading to increased levels of harmony and affinity.

Breathing dominates human physical functions (for obvious reasons!) and therefore it is one of the most powerful aspects to match and deepen rapport quickly. Slowing breathing is a fundamental aspect of relaxation techniques and hypnotherapy (which many coaches use in some form) and changing breathing rate and depth in others is a useful way of changing their state. Laughter and standing up out of a chair can both achieve this quickly.

An important principle of rapport is pacing before leading. Pacing enables the coach to be client centred. Leading can be helpful if the client is in an un-resourceful state. If it would be helpful for a client to relax, the coach firstly need to enter their client's state in some way, using their physiology. Maybe they are tapping their foot anxiously and are sat up straight, so the coach could sit up straight too and tap their finger quietly on the table to match the rhythm of their tapping foot. Subtlety is key, otherwise they will think the coach a bit odd or even rude and therefore resist efforts to engage. To test if they have established rapport, the coach will then change their physiology (maybe shift in their seat) and see if the client follows their lead. If they do, rapport is deepening, which will support the coaching relationship.

With most coaching relationships, there won't be a big need to consciously work with rapport, although it is a useful area to work at in all relationships. Occasionally a client can be more resistant or difficult in some way, or maybe they are completely different to the coach in personality and interests. This is when deliberately working at rapport can be supportive, as long as the coach doesn't overdo it so that their efforts are consciously noticed. This could annoy the client or be unconsciously received as being a bit weird or fake, creating unease at some level and reducing trust.

Reflection is where the coach repeats back to their client what they have heard, to check both the client's understanding and theirs. Reflection is different to *summarising* and *paraphrasing* as it uses the words the client has used, even if it doesn't always make grammatical sense.

Reflective practice is part of continuous learning. A reflective coach will assess their thoughts and actions and then identify learning and development needs.

Reframing The coach can help the client to consider something in a new way by re-framing. A well-known re-frame would be to firstly describe a glass as half empty and then re-frame that glass to half full. Nothing has changed, but something is different. There are many different types of reframing patterns and they all work with the aim of opening up new possibilities.

Regulated Qualifications Framework is the UK system for managing qualifications regulated by *Ofqual.* The RQF indexes qualifications based on their level and size. The higher the qualification, the greater the complexity and difficulty of the skills and knowledge associated with the qualification. There are 8 levels in total. See *accreditation* for more detail about coaching qualifications.

Relationship power can be defined as any type of dominance over the client. The personal values and philosophy of the coach are important factors as even a self-aware coach may be unaware of their hidden intentions regarding power. Power is present in all relationships and reflects the ability to influence others and/or to resist the activities of others. French and Raven (1968) consider there to be a six tier model of social power:

- legitimate – the natural and appropriate hierarchy between coach and client (and possibly the commissioner of the coaching or a senior manager) based on the skills and experience that the coach brings to the relationship
- expert – the coach imposes their knowledge and expertise on the client
- reward – giving the client what they want in exchange for the coach receiving something they want – an example could be finishing early because the client has worked hard - rewards can be given or withheld

- coercive – forcing the client to do something and possibly using punishment if it's not done - this is an abusive power which might be combined with one or more of the other types
- nutrient – inappropriately withholding information or knowledge from the client (or drip-feeding), even when they need it or want it
- referent – where the client wants to be like their coach and have put them on a pedestal in some way.

Subtle examples of negative power in a coaching relationship include the coach:
- imposing their expertise or authority
- controlling the degree of challenge and pace of progress
- having line management responsibilities
- choosing an activity or approach with little time for explanation or objections
- interpreting the coaching conversation without clarifying
- taking responsibility for solutions
- instructing or advising
- seeking praise or flattery.

Other abuses of power include sexual relationships and physical or mental abuse.

It is important to be honest about any of the above situations and discuss potential pitfalls and seek agreement about how to coach. Either the coach or the client could be unaware of dominating behaviour and its possible effect on the dynamics of the coaching relationship. Ultimately, the client is giving permission for the coach to have legitimate power over them and can walk away from the relationship. Transparency, contracting and self-awareness will support the coach to manage the relationship power appropriately.

Representational systems – see *senses*

Resistance is more likely to present itself where coaching has been suggested or imposed, rather than where someone has requested a coach and is therefore more likely to fully engaged in the ethos and process. Some factors that create resistance include:
- limiting beliefs
- fear
- old habits and patterns
- ignorance.

Resistance from a client during coaching may present itself in the following ways:
- getting stuck or presenting barriers
- ambivalence, sulkiness or reluctance to take action
- opposition to conscious thought about the goal or problem
- becoming angry or defensive
- seeking clarity, suggestions or advice
- diverting the conversation with unnecessary detail or over-long stories
- asking the coach questions to divert the focus of attention from themselves
- reluctance to engage with feelings or emotion

- failing to complete agreed actions
- repeated re-scheduling or cancellation of appointments.

Some argue that resistance is a sign that the coach has failed to establish rapport with the client, so this could be a potential area for improvement. Here are some other ways in which resistance to coaching can be overcome, both with individuals and across organisations:

- explain what coaching is and what it isn't - a better understanding of the process
- present the benefits, including measurable return on investment and research findings
- use coaching for high performers as well as for addressing problems
- create a clear induction or contracting process
- clarify confidentiality
- help a client to notice their resistance and as the coach remain non-judgemental
- ask *Socratic questions.*

RESOLVE is a model created by Dr Richard Boldstad from his therapeutic work with post-traumatic stress disorder in Sarajevo in the late 1990s. The model is useful in any coaching situation in order to support people to make the changes they want in the way that they want. Here is a summary:

- resourceful state for the coach – know that change is possible
- establish rapport – pace the client and develop empathy (based on respect for their challenges and ability) and trust

- specify the outcome – assess the situation and set goals
- open up the client's model of the world – help them to recognise their old or current situation, access their own inner resources and generate new strategies
- lead the client towards their outcome – use appropriate tools, techniques or methods
- verify the change – monitor and review progress, with the client identifying the change that has occurred
- ecological exit – the coaching process is complete when the client is able to continue on their own with an awareness of how their future has changed and the wider impacts of this.

Return on investment (ROI) can be calculated where costs are known and the monetary value of coaching can be measured. ROI is notoriously difficult to calculate in coaching situations as many of the benefits are behavioural or attitudinal, making them hard to quantify. (see also *evaluation*). If intended outcomes and numerical measures of success are clearly in place before coaching begins, ROI becomes more measurable and can be calculated using the following formula:

ROI = (coaching benefits / coaching costs) × 100%

Ss

Satir positions (Bandler & Grinder 1989) are five useful types of body language, both in terms of noticing the subtle communication messages of another person and also their deliberate use as a coach for generating rapport or different states within a client. Here is a quick summary of the five Satir positions, which can be adapted for sitting or standing:

- placater – for calmness, confidence or making requests – hands palm upwards, balanced and forward-facing body position which is open and relaxed
- blamer – for exposing problems or issues - pointing with a finger and often leaning forwards
- distracter – for diffusing situations or creating fun – smiling and energising with hands and arms, irregular and off-centre movements
- leveller – for honesty and calmness – hands palm down, symmetrical, solid, relaxed and grounded posture.
- sequencer – for logic, steps and order – moving whole hand (not just the finger) from side to side along a horizontal plane whilst talking
- computer – for thinking and considering – backwards, reserved posture, with maybe crossed arms or legs and the chin on the hand or fingers.

Virginia Satir (a family therapist in the 1970s and 80s) noticed that the leveller position is the least stressful to experience, both for yourself and others who are in your company. Unlike other approaches to rapport, it is more helpful to mismatch these body language categories with another person. The leveller position is the only one that should be routinely matched for helping to generate rapport. For example, two distracters matching each other could be chaotic together and two blamers could argue.

Saville Wave is set of personality and ability profiling tools, which reports on focus styles or professional styles. It is used to identify talents, motives and cultural preference and for predicting performance and potential. Specialist training and licensing is required to administer the Saville Wave profiles.

Senses People take in information through the five senses or *modalities* (sight, sound, touch, smell and taste). This is sometimes described as VAK (visual, auditory and kinesthetic) or *VAKOG*, where olfactory (smell) and gustatory (taste) factors have been included. Paying attention to how your client makes 'sense' of their world can be powerful information as you can use it to build *rapport*. VAKOG are sometimes called the five representational systems.

The first step is to pay attention to the words the client is using, as they will give clues about their preferred sense at that moment. Some brief examples of sensory language (predicates) are shown in the table below. When the coach has identified the dominant sense, they can adapt their language and match the client with similar words from the same sensory group(s). Their communication is then likely to make more sense at the unconscious level.

V	A	K	O	G
bright	accent	run	scent	flavour
bird's eye view	articulate	walk	stink	sweet
perceive	ask	grip	whiff	mouth-watering
perspective	call on	slipped my mind	reek	succulent
see eye-to-eye	tell me	smooth	fresh idea	chewy
tunnel vision	same wavelength	warm	smell a rat	no appetite for it
view	living in harmony	get in touch	fishy situation	sour
watch	humming	sharp tongue	nose for the	juicy idea
see what I mean	double Dutch	surfing the web	business	spicy
looking closely	turn a deaf ear	feel it in my bones	sniff out the	bitter pill to
a hazy notion	that rings a bell	tension in the air	problem	swallow
blind spot	music to my ears	warm-hearted		sweet person
show me	on a good note	project is running		an acid comment
look back on this				

Figure 9 - Examples of Predicates

Sensory acuity is the skill of noticing the smaller clues or cues in the physiology of communication. This includes:

- skin tone and colour
- tone and tempo of the voice
- breathing patterns
- changes to the lips, jaw and eyes
- micro-expressions
- posture, movement and muscle changes.

Scaling is where a numerical (e.g. a scale of 1 to 10) is used to help a client identify

- where they are now and where they want to be
- how they are progressing towards a goal.

Skills required of coaches are many and varied, as this A-Z guide demonstrates. Different coaches will prefer different approaches, methodologies and styles of coaching, all of which are underpinned by a set of core skills, listed here and described in more detail under their individual entries in this book:

- *rapport*
- *listening*
- *questioning*
- *reflecting*
- *clarifying*.

Silence in coaching means various things. The coach can notice their self-talk and turn it down or off. This might include planning solutions or solving problems for the client rather than engaging with enhanced listening skills where the coach remains curious and open. Being *in the moment* and trusting instincts (internal prompts) help create silence.

Time for the client to think, with comfortable silence, is important. The most powerful statements or best ideas often pop out after a longer pause. Silence allows the client to talk to themselves (internal dialogue), process ideas and overcome their objections.

Sixteen Personality Factors (16PF) is a profiling tool that reveals potential, confirms suitability and helps identify development needs, both professionally and personally. It is an accurate predictor of behaviour and potential and is used in both recruitment and personal development. A licence is required to administer the tool. The 16 personality traits were developed by Raymond Catell in the 1940s and are based on the big 5 personality traits of:

- openness
- conscientiousness

- extraversion
- agreeableness
- neuroticism.

SMART (Doran 1981) is an acronym to support goals and objectives so that they demonstrate the following qualities (alternative wording shown):

- specific
- measurable
- assignable (achievable / attainable)
- realistic (relevant)
- time-related

Here are some other SMART acronyms:
- SMARTER – *evaluated* and *reviewed* added as two extra steps at the end. Other alternatives include extending / exciting / ethical or rewarded / recorded.
- SMARTTA – in this version, *trackable* and *agreed* are the last two steps

Socratic questions are a critical thinking tool. The questions challenge accuracy and completeness of thinking in a way that acts to move people towards their ultimate goal. There is a taxonomy of 6 types of question (Paul 1990), designed to:
- clarify what the other person means
- probe assumptions
- investigate the logic, reasons and evidence the other person is using

- examine viewpoints and perspectives
- investigate implications and consequences
- get to the root of the other person's questions – questions about questions.

Solution Focus (SF) approach came originally from the development of new family therapy approaches in the USA in the late 1970s, where instead of analysing problems, therapists asked questions that focused on building solutions in the simplest and easiest way. SF firstly reframes a problem as a future goal and then puts in place steps and resources to achieve the goal. Here are a few examples of SF questions:

- Describe some ways you could start to move towards creating this solution
- What are your thoughts about this solution?
- What impact is thinking about this solution having on you?

SPECIFY is a goal setting acronym (source unknown):

- sensory specific – what will you see/hear/feel when you have this outcome?
- positive language – state the goal in terms of what you want, not what you don't want
- ecological - what else will change when you have this outcome? What situations do you want this outcome in and what situations do you not want it to affect?
- choice - does this outcome increase your choices?
- initiated by self - what will you personally need to do to achieve this?
- first step - identified and achievable.

- your inner or external resources are identified.

Stakeholders are the people, teams or organisations that are affected by (or interested in) coaching activity. Stakeholders can be internal to the organisation or client relationship, or external. Stakeholders can be primary (have a direct connection to the coaching that is taking place) or secondary (an indirect connection). A stakeholder may gain or lose from coaching. Some stakeholders may need to be involved in *contracting*, such as the line manager of the coaching client or a learning and development specialist.

STRIDE is a coaching model (Thomas & Smith 2004):
- strengths – review the client's strengths and keep a resourceful mind-set
- targets – agree the focus (goal or issue) and explore the motivation
- real situation – the current reality and the limiting beliefs
- ideas – weighing up the options and creativity
- decision - selecting the most appropriate option to move forward
- evaluation – explore commitment to action right now and review of progress at a later stage.

STOKeRS is a contracting model (3D Coaching):
- subject - what are we here to talk about?
- time - how long do we have?
- outcome - where are we heading?
- know - how will you know that the conversation has achieved a difference?

- e (silent)
- role - how are we going to work together to do this?
- start - where shall we start?

Summarising is when the coach gives an account of what they have heard from a client in their own (the coach's) words. Sometimes the coach uses the client's words in order to preserve the meaning. No meaning is given in the summary, but instead the coach simply sums up the main points. (See also *paraphrasing* and *reflecting*).

Supervision is a space and time for reflection on coaching practice. This area of coaching is growing rapidly, with the first books on supervision being written as recently as 2006. Supervision can be described as 'the process by which a coach with the help of a supervisor, can attend to understanding better both the client system and themselves as part of the client-coach system, and by doing so transform their work and develop their craft' (Hawkins & Smith 2006). The seven-eyed supervision model (Hawkins 1985) covers the:

- client's system
- coach's interventions
- relationship between the coach and client
- coach
- supervisory relationship
- supervisor self-reflection
- wider context.

SWOT is an acronym for Strengths, Weaknesses, Opportunities, and Threats. The SWOT analysis model came from the research conducted at Stanford Research Institute in the 1960s (Edmund P. Learned et al). SWOT stemmed from the need to find out why corporate planning sometimes failed. The research was to find out what could be done about such failure. The original research team (funded by the Fortune 500 companies) interviewed 5,000 managers at 1,000 companies over nine years using these categories:

- good in the present is satisfactory
- good in the future is an opportunity
- bad in the present is a fault
- bad in the future is a threat.

This was called a SOFT analysis. At a seminar in Zurich in 1964, Urick and Orr changed the F (fault) to a W (weakness), and it has stuck as that; soFt to sWot.

Symbolic Modelling (Penny Tompkins and James Lawley 2000) is an adaptation of David Grove's *clean* language for coaching. By using specific *clean* questions, a coach can begin to replicate the client's experience in their own mind. This coaching approach is totally client led and therefore the coach has minimal influence on the client. The role of the coach is to support the client to explore their metaphor (of the issue or goal) and the coach has no involvement in interpreting or guiding.

Sympathetic nervous arousal (SNA) is the flight or fight response that is partly driven by adrenalin (to sharpen the senses) and cortisol (to increase blood pressure and blood sugars and suppresses the immune system) in order to boost energy and muscle performance. As chemical levels rise, SNA can easily stimulate stress and be responsible for flight or fight responses. The focus of attention narrows (tunnel vision at its extreme), spontaneity reduces, focus on negativity increases and memories, skills and learning are less accessible.

Coaching will have less impact if a client is experiencing a level of SNA, which can often be the case when they arrive at the start of the coaching session. They may be in the middle of a busy day, just left a difficult meeting or had trouble parking their car, all of which will trigger normal day-to-day SNA responses. Some clients will be facing more extreme challenges or difficulties, in which case the SNA response might be more evident. Taking extra time to establish *rapport* and helping a client to relax may be important at the start of a coaching session in order to create the optimum learning environment. Coaching may not be appropriate if SNA is high, so there should be the flexibility (and contract arrangements) to postpone a coaching session or instead use the allocated time differently (mentoring, advising, therapy or counselling depending on the skills set of the coach).

The opposite of sympathetic nervous arousal is *parasympathetic nervous arousal*.

Systemic coaching gives priority to the system to which the client belongs. When coaching a client there will be an impact on their personal development and effectiveness. This will in turn have an impact on colleagues and the team, plus other human systems with which the client has a relationship. Measuring results may include team and organisational performance measures, in addition to individual performance and goals achieved. In system coaching the focus is on relationships and human dynamics.

Tt

Team coaching applies coaching principles to develop the collective capability of a team. The focus shifts away from personal and individual skills or behaviours and places attention on the collective communication, relationships and attributes of the team.

Technique is the skill, capability and ability of a coach to use a tool. This will be affected by learning, practical experience and the development of expertise.

Telephone coaching is a great way to coach when geographical distance is a barrier. Telephone coaching is normally quicker and more focused compared to a face to face meeting, with between 30 and 60 minutes being ideal. Most coaches would probably agree that face to face coaching is easier in terms of establishing a relationship quickly as it is easier to build rapport and trust through verbal and non-verbal communication combined. Telephone coaching requires a different set of tools and approaches from the coach. The most obvious missing element is visual information. This can be overcome by asking the client to describe where they are (and vice versa) and ask them to articulate their physiological responses during the coaching as appropriate. Using a web cam can help, with Skype and Facetime both being popular on-line platforms for this. File sharing software can support real-time note taking. Experienced telephone coaches report that the lack of visual information makes no difference and can actually help, as the additional anonymity can encourage the client to be more open. Professional telephone coaching will include all the elements of a face to face coaching session, such as:

- a contract which reflects the different coaching approach over the phone
- a clear appointment time and calling arrangements
- a clear end time and tracking the conversation using a model such as GROW.

TetraMap is a behavioural profiling tool from New Zealand which uses nature as a metaphor, with the elements of earth, air, fire and water as descriptors. Certification is required and the tool can be administered with individuals and teams.

Thalamus is the area of the brain that directs sensory information (visual, auditory, kinaesthetic, olfactory and gustatory – see also *senses*) to different parts of the *neocortex*.

Therapy offers a safe, confidential place to talk about life and anything that may be confusing, painful or uncomfortable. It allows the client to talk with someone who is trained to listen attentively and to help them improve things (BACP 2017).

Tools are used in coaching to produce a result. Examples of tools are psychometrics, questions, feedback and scorecard exercises. The use and impact of a coaching tool will be affected by the coach's technique.

Transactional analysis (TA) is a model of communication (Berne 1964) based on adult, parent and child relationships (the three *ego states*):

- parent – assert control, nurture, create dependency
- adult – the best role for the coach
- child – looking for sympathy, admiration, seeking attention.

The coach and the client can both recognise their own patterns of thought, feeling and behaviour using this model, so it is useful for examining the boundaries of the coaching relationship (contracting) and the behaviours within it, as well as for supporting the client to explore their relationships, dilemmas, issues and goals. TA has three core principles:

- everyone is OK – this is a position of respect and regard for self and others
- everyone can think and therefore find solutions to problems
- anyone can change.

Transference It is natural to make assumptions about other human beings and the coach can unconsciously behave in a certain way towards the client as a result of past experiences and learning. Transference is where old issues from the past emerge in new relationships and Freud wrote extensively about this in the early twentieth century. A coach can unwittingly create negative or positive relationship states in their client, based on prior experiences and relationships. Trust and professional affection are useful, whereas dominance and dependence aren't. A good phrase to summarise transference is 'who you are is how you coach'. The applications to coaching are extensive, so here are a few useful tips:

- preparing to meet a client for the first time – notice your instinctive responses to that person and what that might mean for the quality of the coaching relationship
- notice signs that your client is becoming dependent upon you or looking up to you in an idealised way as this could indicate signs of your role being that of a parent (support) or boss (authority) for example, rather than a coach – avoid supporting this by praising their achievements as their own, so that the responsibility for success lies firmly with their actions and not your coaching
- notice signs of ego getting in the way and shift the emphasis back to working for the client rather than kudos for yourself

Counter transference is when the client (or the past history of the coach) unconsciously creates a state within the coach. For example, a client might remind the coach of someone and the coach starts to react as if the client were that person rather than themselves. The coach might notice reactions of frustration, tiredness or something else that their client evokes within them, without being clear about why this is the case. If the client is starting to become dependent on the coach or place the coach on a pedestal, the coach might start to live up to that role and then become overly involved (flattered) or overly detached (repulsed). As a coach is it easy to slip into the trap of accepting request for help, support or friendship that goes beyond the coaching interaction.

Experienced coaches will use transference and counter transference as part of their coaching approach. Firstly they will notice their reactions and consider whether or not they need to adjust internally in any way to best support the coaching. Secondly, they might explore what they have experienced with the client: A good question they could ask is "I'm getting a feeling that something is going on here, what might that be?" or name what they are experiencing with a question like "I am feeling frustration, why would that happen?"

Transformative learning and transformational coaching both involve changing perspectives and mind-sets. Sometimes in coaching this is describes as an *'Ah-ha' moment*. This type of coaching often involves revolutionary changes or the development of a new purpose or vision.

Trust creates a comfortable coaching relationship where the client will freely share their thoughts and feelings and show vulnerability. Trust is vital for successful coaching and is a core competency identified by many professional coaching bodies. Trust has to be earned and will grow when the coach:

- is honest and sincere in what you say
- fulfils promises and is reliable
- is congruent – their actions are consistent with their words
- demonstrates a non-judgemental approach
- makes an effort to get to know their client
- shows that they listen.

Uu Vv

Values are an energising and motivating force. Values give goals deep-rooted meaning, so the client will be less likely to give up and be more likely to break through barriers or overcome obstacles and potential failures. For many people, values will surface as a gut instinct or their heart will tell them it's the right way to be going.

Values and beliefs are two terms which are often used as meaning the same thing. They are different concepts and are mutually supportive.

- Values are ideals that we hold to be important and they govern the way we behave, communicate and interact with others.
- Beliefs are more precise concepts that we hold to be true and they are a bit like rules that we set for ourselves.

For example, you might have a strong value around the importance of family in your life and then within this higher ideal or principle, you might have beliefs (rules) about how to achieve this, such as eating together at mealtimes, attending family celebrations whenever it's possible and having a holiday together every year. Values and beliefs determine attitudes and opinions and they are a powerful motivating driver for goals. Values can be inspiring and can also help inform clients about decisions and choices they need or want to make in their lives.

via™ is a coaching model to create *vocational integration and alignment* in coaching conversations. Created by Sara Boas, via™ coaches 'support and challenge leaders to define their own life work, integrate their different roles and relationships and align their personal goals with those of their colleagues, their organisation, and the wider community' (www.boastl.com). The approach focuses on 'developing an alert and courageous coaching presence when working with clients who hold positional power'. Certification is required.

Vision is the ability to perceive the future, including what you want for yourself and the wider impact of this. The principle of vision can be applied to a person, team, an organisation or at other levels in any context. Within a vision there will probably be a sense of smaller steps or *goals*, including long term and short term *aims and objectives*.

VISION is also an acronym and model for working with goals (Smale 2013).

- values
- identity
- stories
- ideas
- options
- next steps.

Vision boards are a popular way to support the *visualisation* of a goal, using the power of the law of attraction. The *law of attraction* states that what enters your life is a result of what you attract into your life. By building a mental picture of what you want, you will attract positive ways to make it happen. A vision board represents things you want to have. The pictures act as a positive emotional connector for your vision.

The reticular activating system (RAS) is the information filtering system in the brain and vision boards work by programming the RAS to tune into things in the environment that can help a person move closer towards their goal. The RAS tags information that is important, stores it within the neurology and then pays attention to it in the environment. An example of this is when a new parent has been programmed to tune in to the small snuffles or whimpers of their baby at night. Maybe you've bought a new coat and all of a sudden you notice other people wearing the same or similar coat. By programming the RAS with a vision board, in theory, the RAS will seek out things in the environment that are in alignment with it.

Visualisation is a way of creating a new experience and a new reference structure that takes a person beyond past or current experiences. It is a mental rehearsal. This means that by visualising having achieved a goal, there exists a guide for the future and how to get there.

Visualisation is widely used by actors, professional sports people and in business. Sometimes called guided imagery, visualisation is safe and relaxing and it can help gain a clearer sense of goals and motivation to achieve them. Visualisation strengthens the connection with a goal and allows the client to imagine the experience of achieving it and the benefits it will bring. Visualisation is supported by the *law of attraction*, meaning that whatever a person is thinking or imagining, they will notice more of and therefore new opportunities and options will present themselves.

Ww

Wisdom access questions (Fortgang 2002) tend to be short and start with 'what'. They are based on the principle that the more specific the question, the more specific the answer. This is a bit like entering key words into a search engine. WAQs start with 'what' and avoid asking 'why', 'who', 'when' and 'how'. Rather than gathering information, WAQs seek specific awareness or solutions. Here are some examples:

- What outcome do you want to reach
- What can you do to improve?
- What do you need to know to understand?
- What would have made a difference?

Well-formed outcome (Bandler & Grinder 1989) is a goal setting structure. Here are the well-formed outcome questions:
- What do you want to see, hear and feel?
- Where do you want this?
- When do you want this?
- Who with?
- How will you know when you've got it?
- What will you see, hear and feel?
- What resources will you need?

The questions should be repeated as many times as possible in order to discover the widest range of possibilities. The best results come from using the questions without any adjustments. The questions are designed to have linguistic patterns that firstly assist with the mental creation of a goal and secondly, presuppose success. The seven questions create an overall representation of a goal that will have increased detail, substance and motivation. It will be well-formed. These questions are useful for a quick coaching session or can be considered by the client for an hour or more.

Wheel of life is a coaching tool that helps the client to see how balanced their life is. It is widely used in life coaching, often at the start of a coaching relationship, as the activity is helpful in determining the most useful or impactful areas for goal setting and change. The wheel of life is easily adapted for any coaching situation, including working with children and teenagers. It works by breaking down the general idea of 'life' or 'work' into smaller components where it is easier to take action. It helps the client to identify if they are placing too much emphasis on one area of their life and neglecting others.

There are normally 8 areas in the wheel, with labels such as recreation, career, money, health, relationships and so on. The client can choose the labels according to the coaching context. Each area is then given a score out of 10 and these scores provide a quick way of comparing how successfully each area is working. It is then easier to identify one area in which to focus the coaching conversation in order to make changes and set worthwhile goals. The wheel can be re-visited to measure progress towards goals and identify new areas for attention. This tool is widely available for free on the internet (both downloadable templates and interactive exercises) and is included in many coaching books and training courses. It is easily adapted for any context.

Why questions seek information, gather detail and go over pervious thoughts. This can perpetuate or deepen the stuck state and the focus remains in the past. The skill of a coach is to reframe clients' questions from 'why' to 'what'. For example, from 'Why aren't I better at this?' to 'What can I do to improve?'

Wise Advocate™ (Schwartz & Gladding) is our inner voice, from the position of being a clear minded observer. The role of the wise advocate is to notice deceptive messages, judgement, emotions or reactions and approach problem solving or goal setting with a nurturing and positive intention. There are four steps to accessing the Wise Advocate (for the coach or the client):

- Step 1: Relabel. Identify the deceptive brain messages (i.e., the unhelpful thoughts, urges, desires and impulses) and put a label on what is happening.
- Step 2: Reframe – ask is this real or is it just my brain? Do I have to believe this?
- Step 3: Refocus – direct your thinking to where you want to go, do something productive or something that is healthy for you.
- Step 4: Revalue – this should start to happen automatically as new habits begin to be created – you start to adapt and function better

Witness A coach is a witness to their client. The coach experiences the words and physiology (body language, breathing, tone of voice and so on) of the client. They are a witness through all three of their senses - not only do they hear (auditory) what the client is saying out loud and see (visual) their movements, the coach will also pick up on emotion and feelings (kinesthetic). It is important that the coach becomes aware of judgements and assumptions that they make as a result of communication from the client, as these will influence the questions that they ask and the way that they ask them. Adopting a witness position (the observer – see also *perceptual positions*) will help the coach resist the temptation to fix, advise, offer opinion or tell their own stories, making it a useful mind-set to adopt.

Xx Yy Zz

The Yerkes–Dodson curve (1908) shows the relationship between urgency, anxiety, fear and performance. Performance increases with physiological or mental arousal up to a point which is sometimes called the 'anxiety sweet spot'. As arousal or stress increases beyond this point, performance falls. Coaching should provide enough challenge to enhance performance, but not beyond the sweet spot so that anxiety or fear sets in and it becomes counter-productive.

Yin Yang coaching seeks to rebalance stresses or opposing factors. According to Taoism, Yin and Yang are two opposing energies that ebb and flow. Some of the different yin (black) and yang (white) characteristics are shown in the lists below, with those that are directly related to coaching shown in italic.

Yin	Yang
Dark	Light
Female	Male
Night	Day
Cold	Hot
Soft	*Hard*
Pull	*Push*
Listening	*Telling*
Asking questions	*Directing*
Building rapport	*Analysing*
Non-directive	*Controlling*
Personal development	*Boundaries*
Ambiguity	*Objectives & measures*

The use of coaching (Yin qualities and skills) in organisations and life can be seen as an extremely useful and are a relatively recent balance to more traditional (and often corporate) styles of Yang energy. Here are some common examples of opposing factors and subsequent balance that clients might seek to achieve:

- self and others
- acceptance and change
- family and friends
- work and life.

Youth coaching supports and empowers teenagers and young adults to overcome problems and achieve goals. There may be additional guidance and legislation that needs to be taken into account when working with young people, depending on their age. This includes background criminal record checks for the coach, plus child protection standards and regulations that will affect the limits of confidentiality and how to deal with disclosure. The ethical boundaries when working with young people, parents and partner organisations such as schools and welfare services will be different and these should be clarified before coaching begins.

References

Arthur, J. (2014). *The Five Limiting Beliefs that Hinder Your Success... and How to Overcome Them.* www.qimacros.com/knowware-articles/five-limiting-beliefs/

Bandler, R., Grinder, J. (1989). *The Structure of Magic 1: A book about language and therapy.* CA: Science & Behavior Books.

Bandler, R., Grinder, J. (1979). *Frogs into Princes: Neuro Linguistic Programming.* Colorado, USA: Real People Press.

Barnlund, D. C. (2008). *A transactional model of communication.* In. C. D. Mortensen (Eds.), Communication theory (2nd ed., pp47-57). New Brunswick, New Jersey: Transaction.

Berman Fortgang, L. (2001). *Living Your Best Life.* NY: Putnam.

British Association for Counselling and Psychotherapy (BACP) www.bacp.co.uk

Berne, E. (1964). *The Games People Play.* New York: Grove Press.

Blakey, J., Day, I. (2012). Challenging Coaching: Going beyond traditional coaching to face the FACTS. London: Nicholas Brealy.

Bolstad, R. (2002). *RESOLVE: A New Model of Therapy.* Carmarthen, UK: Crown House.

Boyatzis, R., Jack, A. (2010). *Coaching with compassion can 'light up' human thoughts.* Case Western Reserve University.

Buckley, A. (2010). Coaching and Mental Health. In Cox, E., Bachkirova, T., Clutterbuck, D. (Eds.), *The complete handbook of coaching.* Thousand Oaks, CA: Sage.

Buzan, T. (1974). *Mind Mapping, use your head.* London: BBC Books.

McGurk, J. (2010). *Real World Coaching Evaluation: A guide for practitioners*. UK: CIPD

Cox, E., Bachkirova T., Clutterbcuk D. (2010). *The Complete Handbook of Coaching*. London, UK: Sage.

Dilts, R. (1994). *Strategies of Genius*. US: Meta Publications.

Dilts, R.B, Epstein, T.A. (1995). *Dynamic Learning*. California: Meta Publications.

Doran, G. T. (1981). *There's a S.M.A.R.T. way to write management's goals and objectives*. Management Review, Volume 70, Issue 11(AMA FORUM), pp. 35–36.

Dweck, C. S. (2006). *Mindset: The new psychology of success*. New York: Random House

Edmund P. Learned et al, in 'Business194 Policy, Text and Cases' (1969).

Fitts, P.M., & Posner, M.I. (1967). *Human performance*. Belmont, CA: Brooks Cole.

French, J.R.P. and Raven, B. (1968). *The Bases of Social Power*. In D. Cartwright and A. Zander (editors), Group Dynamics, Harper and Row.

Fortgang, L. B. (2002). *Living Your Best Life*. New York: Penguin Putnam.

Gallese, V., Fadiga, L., Fogassi, L. & Rizzolatti, G. (1996). Action recognition in the premotor cortex. Brain, 119,593-609.

Gardiner, H. (1983). Frames of Mind: The Theory of Multiple Intelligences. New York: Basic Books.

Goleman, D. (1996). *Emotional Intelligence: Why It Can Matter More Than IQ*. New York: Bantam Books.

Grant, A. M. (2012). *Making Positive Change: A Randomized study comparing Solution-Focused vs. Problem-Focused Coaching Questions*. Journal of Systemic Therapies, 31 (2), 21 – 35.

Grinder, J., de Lozier, J. (1987). *Turtles all the Way Down: Prerequisites to Personal Genius*. California, Scotts Valley.

Gurjer, J. (2017) https://coachcampus.com/coach-portfolios/coaching-models/jahnavi-gurjer-d-i-c-e/ accessed 18.8.2017

Hawkins, P. (1985). *Humanistic psychotherapy supervision. A Conceptual Framework: Self and society.* European Journal of Humanistic Psychology, *13*(2): 69-77.

Hawkins, P., Smith, N. (2006). *Coaching, mentoring and organizational consultancy:* UK: Oxford University Press.

Hofstede, G., Hofstede, G. J. (2004). *Cultures and Organizations, Software of the Mind*. UK: McGraw-Hill Professional.

Jackson, P. Z., McKergow, M. (2006). *The Solutions Focus: Making Coaching and Change SIMPLE*. London: Nicholas Brealey.

Ishikawa, K. (1968). *Guide to Quality Control*. Tokyo: JUSE.

Karpman, S. (1968). Fairy tales and script drama analysis. Transactional Analysis Bulletin, 7(26), 39-43.

Kirkpatrick, D. L. (1976). *Evaluation of Training*. In R. L. Craig (Ed.), Training and Development Handbook. A Guide to Human resource Development (pp. 181-191). New York: MacGraw-Hill.

Knowles, M. (1978). *The adult learner: a neglected species.* Houston TX: Gulf.

Kolb, D. (1984). *Experiential learning: Experience as the source of learning and development.* Englewood Cliffs NJ: Prentice Hall.

Lawley, D. J., Tompkins, P. L. (2000). *Metaphors in Mind: Transformation Through Symbolic Modelling.* London: The Developing Company Press.

Learned, E. P., Christiansen, C. R., Andrews, K., Guth, W. D. (1969) *Business Policy, Text and Cases.* US: R. D. Irwin

Luft, J., Ingham, H. (1955). *The Johari window, a graphic model of interpersonal awareness.* Proceedings of the western training laboratory in group development. Los Angeles: UCLA.

Maslow, A.H. (1943). *A theory of human motivation.* Psychological Review 50 (4) 370–96.

Mehrabian, A., and Ferris, S.R. (1967). Inference of Attitudes from Nonverbal Communication in Two Channels, *Journal of Consulting Psychology*, 31, 3, 48-258.

Marston, William M. (1928). *Emotions of Normal People.* K. Paul, Trench, Trubner & Co. ltd. New York: Harcourt, Brace and Company.

Mezirow, J. (1990). *Fostering critical reflection in adulthood: A guide to transformative and amancipatory learning.* San Fransisco, CA: Jossey-Bass.

Murphy, M. (2010). *Hard Goals : The Secret to Getting from Where You Are to Where You Want to Be.* US: McGraw-Hill.

Paul, R. (1990). *Critical Thinking: How to Prepare Students for a Rapidly Changing World*. Santa Rosa, CA: Foundation for Critical Thinking.

Pendleton, D., Scofield, T., Tate, P., Havelock, P. (1984).*The consultation: an approach to learning and teaching.* Oxford: Oxford University Press.

Pinker, S. (1999). *How the Mind Works*. New York: Oxford University Press.

Rohnke, K. (1989). *Cowstails and Cobras II*. Iowa: Kendal Hunt Publishing.

Rose, C. (1985). *Accelerated Learning*. UK: Accelerated Learning Systems Ltd.

Rotter, J. B. (1954). *Social Learning and Clinical Psychology*. New York: Prentice-Hall.

Senay, I., Albarracín, D., & Noguchi, K. (2010). *Motivating Goal-Directed Behavior Through Introspective Self-Talk: The Role of the Interrogative Form of Simple Future Tense*. Psychological Science 21(4), 499-504.

Schramm, W. (1954). *How communication works.* In W. Schramm (Ed.), The process and effects of communication (pp. 3-26). Urbana, Illinois: University of Illinois Press.

Schutz, W.C. (1958). *FIRO: A Three Dimensional Theory of Interpersonal Behavior*. New York: Holt, Rinehart, & Winston.

Schwartz, J. M., Gladding, R. (2011): *You Are Not Your Brain: The 4-Step Solution for Changing Bad Habits, Ending Unhealthy Thinking, and Taking Control of Your Life*. New York: Avery.

Shannon, C. E., & Weaver, W. (1949). The mathematical theory of communication. Urbana, Illinois: University of Illinois Press.

Smale, C. M. (2103). *Transform your goals with VISION*. UK: Clare M Smale

Thomas, G. *Skill instruction in outdoor leadership: A comparison of a direct instruction model and a discovery-learning model*. Australian Journal of Outdoor Education, 11(2), 10-18, 2007.

Thomas, W. and Smith, A. (2010). *Coaching Solutions: practical ways to improve performance in education*. London: Bloomsbury.

Wahl, C., Scriber, C., Bloomfield, B.. (2008). *On becoming a leadership coach: a holistic approach to coaching excellence*. New York: Palgrave Macmillan.

Whitmore, J. (2002). *Coaching for Performance*. London: Nicholas Brealey Publishing Ltd.

Whitworth, L., Kimsey-House, H., Sandahl, P. (1988). *Co-active Coaching: New Skills for Coaching People Towards Success in Work and Life*. Palo Alto, CA: Davies-Black.

Zenger, J., Stinnett, K. (2010). *The Extraordinary Coach: How the Best Leaders Help Others Grow*. US: McGraw-Hill.

Want to know more?

Why not invite Clare Smale as a speaker for your next conference or event?

clare@inspired2learn.co.uk

www.inspired2learn.co.uk

Coaching for your organisation

Clare runs workshops and training events and speaks at conferences and events. Coaching can be tailored to suit your needs and adapted for working with teams and professional coaches or leaders at all levels. Your workshop or training will be interactive and engaging and will include resources and materials to keep.

Coaching courses are formally recognised and certificated by the Institute of Leadership and Management:

- Development programmes
- Level 3 Award and Certificate in Coaching and / or Mentoring
- Level 5 Certificate and Diploma in Coaching and Mentoring
- Level 7 Certificate and Diploma in Executive Coaching and Mentoring

Gain a coaching qualification

Approved
Centre

Would you like to learn how to coach and develop your coaching style at work?

Maybe you would like to become a professional coach within your organisation or independently.

Our distance learning option for coaching qualifications has become increasingly popular, especially for existing coaches who would like accreditation and a formal qualification for their CV that is nationally recognised.

Clare can support you through your qualification with either a taught programme of workshops or via distance learning. You will get plenty of help and advice by email and telephone, plus access to a large range of on-line resources whenever you want them. Clare will help you to design the timescales and learning styles to suit your needs and experience and you can start any time you like.

- Level 3 Award and Certificate in Coaching and / or Mentoring
- Level 5 Certificate and Diploma in Coaching and Mentoring
- Level 7 Certificate and Diploma in Executive Coaching and Mentoring

Coaching for Schools

Clare taught in secondary schools for 13 years before establishing a successful business training and developing others. She has continued to work extensively in schools and with teachers. Here is a selection of what she can offer for your school through workshops, INSET days, coaching, conferences or facilitation:

- Coaching and mentoring skills: training and accreditation
- Personal coaching at all levels
- Coach Mark accreditation
- Speaking at conferences and events.
- Interpersonal skills and personal development events
- Coachmark support and assessment – achieve a nationally recognised quality mark for coaching culture and practices in your school

Learn to coach

Enhance your coaching skills

Clare runs open courses, workshops and training events during the year. The training is interactive and engaging and includes resources and materials to keep.

Coaching courses can be formally recognised and certificated by the ILM:

- Level 3 Award and Certificate in Coaching and / or Mentoring
- Level 5 Certificate and Diploma in Coaching and Mentoring
- Level 7 Certificate and Diploma in Executive Coaching and Mentoring

www.inspired2learn.co.uk

Clare's Coaching Cards - coach yourself or others

- coach individuals or teams

- have meaningful conversations

- create a compelling future

- develop goals

- solve problems

- identify steps and actions

- have fun and be inspired

Each pack of Coaching Cards contains

- 55 coaching questions that can be used in a wide variety of conversations at home, work, in business or elsewhere

- 55 original photographs to stimulate thinking, problem solving and create engaging coaching conversations

Buy your cards at

www.inspired2learn.co.uk

About the author

Clare Smale is a highly respected coach, trainer and speaker.

Clare has over 20 years' experience of supporting people to be at their best. Before founding inspired2learn with her husband in 2002, she was a teacher and leader in three 11-18 comprehensive schools. Clare has spent the last twelve years as a trainer and performance coach for a wide variety of private and public sector organisations. Clare's particular interests are in helping leaders and managers to tackle the challenges associated with managing change and team working, with a focus on personal development and resilience.

Clare is a trained and accredited coach, NLP Master Practitioner and NLP Trainer. Over the years, she has helped thousands of people achieve their goals. Her first book, *Transform your Goals with VISION*, was published in 2013 and is available in hard copy and for Kindle.

Clare spends much of her time training coaches, including gaining a recognised qualification in Coaching and / or Mentoring with the Institute of ILM. Inspired2learn is a registered ILM Centre with approval to deliver a range of ILM programmes and qualifications. Just get in touch to find out more via www.inspired2learn.co.uk.